LOBA

OTHER BOOKS BY DIANE DI PRIMA

This Kind of Bird Flies Backward

Dinners and Nightmares

The New Handbook of Heaven

Poets' Vaudeville

Seven Love Poems from the Middle Latin

Haiku

New Mexico Poem

Earthsong

Hotel Albert

Memoirs of a Beatnik

L.A. Odyssey

The Book of Hours

Kerhonkson Journal

Revolutionary Letters

The Calculus of Variation

Loba, Part I

Freddie Poems

Brass Furnace Going Out

Selected Poems

Loba, Part II

The Loba As Eve

Loba: Parts I–VIII

Wyoming Series

The Mysteries of Vision

Pieces of a Song

Seminary Poems

The Mask Is the Path of the Star

LOBA

Diane di Prima

PENGUIN POETS

PENGUIN BOOKS

Published by the Penguin Group
Penguin Putnam Inc., 375 Hudson Street,
New York, New York 10014, U.S.A.
Penguin Books Ltd, 27 Wrights Lane,
London W8 5TZ, England
Penguin Books Australia Ltd, Ringwood,
Victoria, Australia
Penguin Books Canada Ltd, 10 Alcorn Avenue,
Toronto, Ontario, Canada M4V 3B2
Penguin Books (N.Z.) Ltd, 182–190 Wairau Road,
Auckland 10, New Zealand
Penguin India, 210 Chiranjiv Tower, 43 Nehru Place,
New Delhi 11009, India

Penguin Books Ltd, Registered Offices:
Harmondsworth, Middlesex, England

Loba, Part One, published in the United States of America
by Capra Press 1973
Loba, Part Two, published by Eidolon Editions 1976
Loba as Eve published by Phoenix Book Shop 1977
Loba, Parts I–VIII, published by Wingbow Press 1978
This expanded edition published in Penguin Books 1998

Some of the poems in Book II appeared in *Pieces of a Song* (City Lights, 1990), *The
Mask Is the Path of the Star* (Thinker Review Press, 1993), and in the following
periodicals: *Bay Area Women's News, Black Ace, Earth's Daughters, Ergo!, First Intensity,
Intent, Lips, Long News in the Short Century, Psychological Perspectives, Taos Review,* and
Tule Review.

LIBRARY OF CONGRESS CATALOGING-IN-PUBLICATION DATA
Di Prima, Diane.
Loba/Diane di Prima.
p.   cm.—(Penguin poets)
Includes previously published Loba: parts I–VIII with new material.
ISBN 0 14 058.752 7
I. Title.
PS3507.I68L6   1998
811'.54—dc21   97–41144

Printed in the United States of America
Set in Bembo
Designed by Claire O'Keeffe

Contents

AVE   1

BOOK I

PART 1

"If he did not come apart . . ."   11

"Who will describe the triumph . . ."   11

"And if she bends . . ."   12

"Is she city? . . ."   12

"Signals. Does she stream . . ."   13

"See how her tit drags on the ground."   13

"See the young, black, naked . . ."   14

"see how old woman's tits . . ."   14

"Hush, the old-young woman"   15

"If you do not come apart . . ."   15

SKETCHES OF THE LOBA   16

"How he drew her *down* . . ."   17

THE LOBA DANCES   18

PART 2

"The day lay like a pearl . . ."   23

"where did it"   24

THREE MORE SKETCHES OF THE LOBA   25

"It is still news to her . . ."   26

"Can you, friend, say . . ."   26

"Sometimes she slips sinuous . . ."   27

"when she hoots it makes"   27

"she strides in blue jeans . . ."   28

"And will you hunt the Loba?"   29

LOBA IN CHILDBED   30

THE LOBA SINGS TO HER CUB   33

"HOW DO THE GODS MANIFEST . . ."   34

LOVE SONG OF THE LOBA   35

THE LOBA CONTINUES TO SING   37

PART 3

SOME SHAPES OF THE LOBA   41

Her power is to open what is shut . . .   43

"she is the wind . . ."   45

"she is the scrub oak . . ."   46

"She lay"   47

LITANY   48

THE POET PRAYS TO THE LOBA   49

MADNESS OF THE LOBA   50

DEATH & THE LOBA   52

"Is he in bondage? . . ."   53

"Belili   Ishtar . . ."   54

THE LOBA OLD   55

PART 4

"I am a shadow . . ."   59

CHILDHOOD OF THE LOBA   60

SOME LIES ABOUT THE LOBA   62

FOUR POETS SPEAK OF HER   63

A PAINTING OF THE LOBA   65

DREAM: The Loba Reveals Herself   67

LOBA AS EVE   69

   i am thou & thou art i   71

   and where thou art i am   72

   & in all things am i dispersed   73

   & from wherever thou willst . . .   74

   but in gathering me . . .   75

PART 5

"Helen on the wall"   79

REEDGATHERERS: The Loba North   81

SONG OF THE DREAM-WOLVES   82

LILITH: AN INTERLUDE   83

   "She flies over partitions . . ."   85

   "Whose mouth"   85

   "Diamond, quartz, agate . . ."   86

   "A handful of starchips thrown"   86

   "The horned lady"   86

   "Or is she soft"   87

   "Or she takes yr shape . . ."   87

   "Delicious the flesh she offers . . ."   88

   "You roll, listing thru gummy sheets . . ."   88

   "She sleeps on sheepskins . . ."   89

   "all night long we"   89

   "Oh Lil! You promised me secrets . . ."   90

   "I'm biting at yr leash . . ."   90

   "O taste the"   91

   "crystal pyramid w/ diamond heart"   91

   "She is not Helen . . ."   92

   "Huntress. She in red sari"   93

PERSEPHONE   94

ISEULT ON THE SHIP   95

SONG OF HELOISE   97

PART 6

The Seven Joys of the Virgin

   ANNUNCIATION   101

   VISITATION: Elizabeth & Mary   104

   NATIVITY   107

   FLIGHT INTO EGYPT   109

   THE RUSES: A COYOTE TALE   110

   THE POET, SEEKING HER   111

   THE MARRIAGE AT CANA   112

   JULIANA   113

   RESURRECTION   115

   CORONATION   117

PART 7

"This wolf is black . . ."   123
THE LOBA RECOVERS THE MEMORY
   OF A MARE   125
MY LADY, WE ARE BEING HUNTED   128
GUARDAVIAZ!   129
AND SHE TO TRISTAN   131
"O make Latona white . . ."   133
THE LOBA ADDRESSES THE GODDESS   134
"In whose dream"   135
"Is it She in flame at heart"   136
THE LOBA, IN MAY   137
THE CRITIC REVIEWS LOBA   138
THE LOBA PREPARES AN AMULET FOR HER
   DAUGHTER   139
"But we cant"   140
GUINEVERE   141
"Antlered"   143

PART 8

LOBA, TO APOLLO   147
HYMN: The Other Face   149
REPRISE   150
FOR CAMERON   152
"LIGHT MADE MY BODY TO LIVE . . ."   154
NOW BORN IN UNIQUENESS, JOIN THE COMMON QUEST   155
"and when we have won clear"   156
LILITH OF THE STARS   158

BOOK II
PART 9

THE SECOND DAUGHTER: LI (BRIGHTNESS)   163
LOBA AS KORE IN THE LABYRINTH OF
   HER BEAUTY   165

BELTAIN NOTE   167

AULA LUCIS   168

"Endurance. What remains"   169

"And this is a clearing . . ."   170

COUGAR NIGHT REPORT   171

TAHUTI POEMS   173

  "where he passes . . ."   175

  "Tahuti / Starfire . . ."   176

  "Tahuti. / He-who-prefigures . . ."   176

  "Tahuti. / Wielder of Image . . ."   177

  "No lotus . . ."   178

  "Tahuti, whose spells leap"   179

    He Who Was Not Born from a Lotus   180

  "Human fledgling"   181

PART 10

  SACRED GEOMETRY   185

  "The bull"   192

  SHE WHO   193

  THE LOBA PRIESTESS AS BAG LADY UTTERS

    RAGGED WARNINGS   194

  DEEP LEAP   196

PART 11

Another Part of Loba

"And Loba is Lovha . . ."   205

"Thus Love"   206

  CREVASSE   208

"From the wished universe"   209

"Stealth of thieves"   210

"thus there is"   211

"The sticky nature of"   211

"But in the longhouse"   212

"The body itself is the vector"   213

"To bring the whole form into silence"   213

What does it mean to rot? 214

A NOTE ON THE ABOVE 215

"know the difference between . . ." 216

"the arms (branches" 217

of Loba 218

"the city . . ." 219

The Interloper 220

LOBA: The Winds of Change 221

PART 12

WALPURGIS 225

"THE LOBA COMPARES THE EARTHLY & HEAVENLY MOTHERS 226

THE MASK IS THE PATH OF THE STAR 227

[DREAM OF EMILY DICKINSON AS IMMATERIAL

SURF BREAKING] 234

PARTHENOS 235

PART 13

"The Memory of far things" 241

"chance arrangement . . ." 241

"She has not left me . . ." 242

GWALCHMAI 243

URSA 245

THE LOBA IN BROOKLYN 246

A PART OF THE THOUSAND WAYS TO SAY

GOODBYE 250

SUNWOLF: Beltain 253

HERMETIC ASTRONOMY 255

PART 14

THE LOBA LONGS FOR REMEMBRANCE

IN THE BARDO 263

EROS/ANIMUS 264

HER DREAM 265

"APPARUIT" 266

INANNA: The Epiphany   269

THEOLOGY BECOMES THE BODY POLITIC   269

"Even w/ jewels on her eyes . . ."   270

MEDUSA GAZEBO   271

THE LOBA IN FLANDERS   272

"Is it"   273

BEING IN LOVE WITH DARKNESS   274

"Bears see only"   277

THE STARS SHINE FOR US   278

ISHTAR   280

AUTOUR DE   281

PART 15
KALI-MA

"Because you love the burning grounds"   285

"You are the dancing youth . . ."   286

"My mother is mad . . ."   287

"Oh mind, you have lost the root"   287

"Make me mad, O Mother!"   288

"When will heart lotus bloom"   288

"O the unmatched beauty . . ."   289

"Mother Kali! Madwoman! . . ."   289

"Kali's greatness . . ."   290

"O Mother, put on a robe . . ."   290

"What woman dances on this battleground?"   291

"She is opposed to custom"   291

"Tara's name makes all prosperity vanish."   292

"I try to make an Image of illusion"   293

"She strides on the battlefield . . ."   293

"The Lady is fresh as jasmine"   294

"They call me drunkard . . ."   294

"I draw a circle about me"   295

"I was drawn to this world"   295

"The six systems of philosophy . . ."   296

"The days will pass . . ."   296

PART 16

VISION OF THE HAG, DEVOURED   299

SABBAT REVISITED   300

TSOGYAL   302

Imago Mundi   304

POINT OF RIPENING: Lughnasa   305

REPORT TO APHRODITE (Evening)   308

The girl had brought the weather with her   311

ARIADNE AS STARMAKER   312

PERSEPHONE: Reprise   314

AUTHOR'S NOTE

The Work is, like they say, in "progress".
The author reserves the right to juggle, re-arrange,
cut, osterize, re-cycle parts of the poem in future editions.
As the Loba wishes, as the Goddess dictates.

AVE

O lost moon sisters
crescent in hair, sea underfoot do you wander
in blue veil, in green leaf, in tattered shawl do you wander
with goldleaf skin, with flaming hair do you wander
on Avenue A, on Bleecker Street do you wander
on Rampart Street, on Fillmore Street do you wander
with flower wreath, with jeweled breath do you wander

    footprints
           shining mother of pearl
                      behind you
    moonstone eyes
        in which the crescent moon

with gloves, with hat, in rags, in fur, in beads
under the waning moon, hair streaming in black rain
wailing with stray dogs, hissing in doorways
shadows you are, that fall on the crossroads, highways

jaywalking do you wander
spitting do you wander
mumbling and crying do you wander
aged and talking to yourselves
with roving eyes do you wander
hot for quick love do you wander
weeping your dead

           naked you walk
           swathed in long robes you walk
           swaddled in death shroud you walk
           backwards you walk

```
                    hungry
                    hungry
                    hungry

                shrieking I hear you
                singing I hear you
                cursing I hear you
                praying I hear you

you lie with the unicorn
you lie with the cobra
you lie in the dry grass
you lie with the yeti
you flick long cocks of satyrs with your tongue

        you are armed
        you drive chariots
        you tower above me
        you are small
        you cower on hillsides
        out of the winds

pregnant you wander
barefoot you wander
battered by drunk men you wander

        you kill on steel tables
        you birth in black beds
                fetus you tore out stiffens in snow
                it rises like new moon
                you moan in your sleep
```

digging for yams you wander
looking for dope you wander
playing with birds you wander
chipping at stone you wander

I walk the long night seeking you
I climb the sea crest seeking you
I lie on the prairie, batter at stone gates
calling your names

you are coral
you are lapis and turquoise
your brain curls like shell
you dance on hills

    hard-substance-woman you whirl
    you dance on subways
    you sprawl in tenements
    children lick at your tits

you are the hills, the shape and color of mesa
you are the tent, the lodge of skins, the hogan
the buffalo robes, the quilt, the knitted afghan
you are the cauldron and the evening star
you rise over the sea, you ride the dark

I move within you, light the evening fire
I dip my hand in you and eat your flesh
you are my mirror image and my sister
you disappear like smoke on misty hills
you lead me thru dream forest on horseback
large gypsy mother, I lean my head on your back

I am you
and I must become you
I have been you
and I must become you
I am always you
I must become you

ay-a
ay-a ah
ay-a
ay-a ah ah
maya ma maya ma
om star mother ma om
maya ma ah

BOOK I

It would be very pleasant to die with a wolf woman
It would be very pleasant

A clever man builds a city
A clever woman lays one low

SHI CHING

PART 1

If he did not come apart in her hands, he fell
like flint on her ribs, there was no
middle way, the rocks screamed
in the flowing water; stars dizzy
w/ pain, if he was not
daisies in her soup he was another
nettle in her hair, she stumbled
crazy over the stony path between
slanderous trees; even field mice knew
she called the shots, dimensions
of the obsidian cross he
hung on, singing in the sun, her eyes
cloudy w/ nightmare, she grinned
baring her wolf's teeth. . . .

Who will describe the triumph streaming
out of her pelt, the symphonies
wind carried to her fine nose?
Her walk, graceful but never feline
shoulders moving as she strode
through undergrowth, dew from the ferns
wet her tits, her short, clear barks?

And if she bends, eternally, at tables
at wood tables in factories, fashioning
crosses of silver, this time, inlaid
with jet & abalone, will you meet
her eyes, she raises
her head. . . .

Is she city? Gate she is we know
& has been, but the road
paved w/ white stones? her paws
are cut by it, the lights
blind her, yet she knows, she comes
to it, white porcelain lining
dome of her brain, she flies
to it on broomstick, on gold mandala
platter or calendar, she sits, her tail
curled round her neat white paws. . . .

Signals. Does she stream, in
wind, her nose riding channels
of the seven rays, the planets
vibrating in her brain, the curling
canals of her guts? Strait as
her eyes, her spine
cd be, but it curves, she curves it
around weeds, she lies down
in the sun.

See how her tit drags on the ground.
She steps on it. She *baaaas*.
She keens, as an old black goat, waiting
blow of the ax. Feel head roll on
wet earth, blood spout (fountain)
from neck, strong as column.
See her dance.

See the young, black, naked woman riding
a dead white man. Her hair
greasy, she whips him & he flies
thru the smoky air. Her hand
is in her mouth, she is eating
flesh, it stinks, snakes wind
around her ankles. Her hand
touches the (wet) earth. Her hand
shakes a gourd rattle, she laughs, her fangs
flash white & red, they are set
with rubies.

see how old woman's tits hang down
on that young, lithe body, know the skull
in her hand your own, she eats
your eyes & then your brain. . . .

Hush, the old-young woman
touches you, she is gold, she wears
a peaked cap, vines
grow out of it. Her tongue flicks
at the corners of her mouth. She says
    "The white gold
      almost invisible is made
      from the red-yellow metal, it is
      the Link." Bodies
pass out of hers, doubles
in silver, copper, iron. Glistening. They lick
their lips. They float on out. Her eyes
show waters parting a jungle, her arms
are vines around you, her tongue
is growing in your mouth. She
thrusts a finger deep into your cunt.

If you do not come apart like bread
in her hands, she falls
like steel on your heart. The flesh
knows better than the spirit what the soul
has eyes for. Has she sunk
root in yr watering place, does she look
w/ her wolf's eyes out of your head?

SKETCHES OF THE LOBA

She stood in the dark bar trying
to turn him into a cobra.
To grow those three horns into
the old, familiar hood.

————————

O the soft
red walls she clung to, they held
her only for a second, she came down
in a torrent of blood

————————

It is snowing in the jungle of her pelt,
                         the crystals
Dance in her cavernous nostrils.

How he drew her *down* to pleasure! She left
the flickering ice for the candlelight to watch
him bending his head w/ the weight
of invisible antlers. It was a role
she was tired of playing. In her
mind's eye she saw herself loping across Europe
naked & lean on the beaches, presiding
at gypsy festivals. She glimmered
black & white like some elusive
                              opal. Who wd
brush donkey shit off her skirt, lick
the beach tar off her feet by the flickering
grey seas of the north? In the candlelight she moved
                              her hands, her rings
played, she moved, her face, her mouth, her voice
fell like water on him.

THE LOBA DANCES

She raises
        in flames
                the
city
    it glows about her
                   The Loba
mother wolf &
             mistress
of many
        dances she
treads
     in the severed heads
                 that grow
like mosses
        on the flood
            the city
melts it
      flows past her
treading
      white feet they
curl around
        ashes & the ashes
sing, they chant
        a new
            creation myth

ghoul lips of
                    lovers she
                                    left
like pearls
            in the road
                                    she
dances, see

her eyes
            glow the
                            city
glows dancing
                in them
                                wolf cry you hear
falls
    from the stars
                        the Loba
dances, she
                treads the
salty earth, she
                    does not
                                raise
breath cloud heavenward
                                    her breath
itself
    is carnage.

PART 2

The day lay like a pearl on her lap
she licked at it w/ the edges of her brain
The day shone in her lap like a promise
of lotuses sprouting from warm worm-eaten mud
but the sand under her toes was dry
dry the dust in her hair
dry & smooth her cunt like lapis lazuli
between her legs, close lapis cunt closegrained,
                                    & veined
w/ silver; the day sat
in her fingers like a jewel she turned
in the failing light, the sun
falling into her sea turned
smoky quartz day to a yellow
                          diamond, a topaz
and then to apache tears the starlight
broke on, as on the waves

where did it
come from, were there
any more where it
came from, had she
remembered to
pay for it

rhinestones in her ears shook
sideways, glittering, rattled
a little, she sat down
on the curb, with a small boy
ate a tomato

THREE MORE SKETCHES OF THE LOBA

worldly & smooth as an
ax blade, she
licked her lips

——————

and if she sat, her wet
back curled against wet
granite in the glowing
rainforest dawns

——————

the smooth white stones she gave me
to pay her passage

It is still news to her that passion
could steer her wrong
though she went down, a thousand times
strung out
across railroad tracks, off bridges
under cars, or stiff
glass bottle still in hand, hair soft
on greasy pillows, still it is
news she cannot follow love (his
burning footsteps in blue crystal
snow) & still
come out all right.

Can you, friend, say you never leaned
across her jagged, bloody wrists to blow
her dripping candles out after you spread
a tattered army blanket over
her swollen face?

Sometimes she slips sinuous thru green
transparent waters, flicking her tail
she dries on white rocks watching dolphins
her small breasts rise, point skyward, while she
brushed her dripping, tangled hair. . . .

Is that the laugh
still ringing in your ears?

when she hoots it makes
the little grasses bloom
when she shuffles her soft
worn moccasins. her headdress
    (horns made of corncobs)
rustled as she turned
sideways in the flat light
off pueblo walls. . . .

she strides in blue jeans to the corner
bar; she dances
w/ the old women, the men
light up, they order wine,
sawdust is flying under her feet
her sneakers, thudding soft
her wispy hair falls sometimes
into her face

were it not for the ring of fur
                    around her ankles
just over her bobby socks
                         there's no one
wd ever guess her name. . . .

And will you hunt the Loba?
Fools, will you use
lance, spear or arrow, gun or
boomerang? Think you she can be caught
in nets of love? She rides
the crescent moon like a flat-bottomed boat
in the stormy well o'the sky
Will you fish for her? Do you hope
to wrap you warm in her pelt
for the coming winter?

Do you dream
to chew shreds of her flesh from inside of her skin
turn inside out her gut, suck juice
from her large, dark liver? Will you make a cap
of her stomach, necklace of her spine?

Look, she lies on her back in the sand like a human woman
the huge saguaro cactus bends to her, her love cry
darkens the mesa. Desert air grows black. Now
she rises, like the sun, she flicks
her tail, he is her black raincloud, he is
Señor Peyotl, grinning. Hand-in-hand
they run over the glassy yellow edge
of your horizon. . . .

After her! Whales-tooth & abalone
jingle as you give chase, yr horse
turns to tumbleweed, the mountains
smell of her breath, once again it is written
NOLI ME TANGERE in jewels
across the sky.

LOBA IN CHILDBED

She lay in bed, screaming, the boat
carried her to the heart of the mandala
sweat stuck
hair to her forehead, she
lay back, panting, remembering
it was what she *should* do. Skull boat
carried her to the heart of her womb, red
pulsing eye of her spirit. She saw
soul shine shoaled on rocks, flint edges
of rocky pelvic cage, caught, swirls
of bland liquid eddying round
curls of bright
red-gold hair, she
screamed, for him, for herself, she
tried to open, to widen tunnel, the rock
inside her tried to crack, to chip away
bright spirit hammered at it w/ his
softy foamy head
                        she cried out
bursting from the heart
                                    of the devastated
mandala, skull boat grew wings
                                    she fluttered
thru amniotic seas to draw him on.

          Gold
          swirling sun, gold
          swirling folds of
          kesa, enfolding, blinding
          her opaquer eyes

                    the speck
                    of red alchemic gold
                    caught in black
                    womb spasm
                    struggled weaker
                    toward earthlight
                    she offered.

It was
round stone head monolith
lying in Colombian jungle
tried to articulate, to burst
out of her.

It was
line drawing bird soul
as in hieroglyphs or in
Indian drawing fluttered
down to meet her

Snatches of brief music, unremitting
white pain, his only
signals

———————

Dark cave. Dark forces countering
magic w/ magic. No time
to navigate now; no white
quartz, no lapis, incense, blessed
flowery water. Only
shrill mantra scream, arch

mudra of tossing pain
torture of watching spirit, measured
in pulse beat   from wires tied
to heart of her cunt, center
of her womb. Have the oceanic
presences deserted her?

       She walked moaning
       into dry heart of
       sandstone continent
       snatched pale
       phosphorescing son
       from red cliffs,
       the sun
       flashed like pain
       behind her eyes

————

Was he limp, did he stir
w/ life, did she hear
his soft breath in her ear?

THE LOBA SINGS TO HER CUB

O my mole, sudden & perfect
golden gopher tunneling
to light, o separate(d)
strands of our breath!
                      Bright silver
threads of spirit
                  O quicksilver
spurt of fist, scansion of
unfocussed eyeball,
                      grace of yr
cry, or song, my
cry or
        you lie warm,   wet on the
soggy pelt of my
                hollowed
belly, my
                bones curve up
to embrace you.

HOW DO THE GODS MANIFEST, WHERE DO THEY
HOME AGAIN? SHE SHONE
LIKE A WHITE LIGHT IN THE DARK
NORTHERN FOREST, WOLF-WOMAN AND VALKYRIE RIDING
THE DARK MIST, RIDING
WITH RED SHOUTS OVER THE HILLTOP, HER
LANCE DRIPPING, BLOOD SWELLING
FROM ITS BRASS TIP, OR SHE SWAM
UPSTREAM IN ICY RIVERS, GREEN HER
WHITE PELT UNDER THE FLOWING
WATERS

LOVE SONG OF THE LOBA

O my lord, blue beast
on the pale green snows, see
I have been running to keep up
w/ you
        I have been
                running to find you
my tongue
          scours ice your
                    tracks made
I drink
        hollows of yr steps,
                   I thought
many a dark beast was you only to find
perfume of your fur, bright cloud
of yr breath not there, they are
flesh & clay, heavy dross, they do not
fly
   in the wind,
              see I have flown
to you, do you
             lurk in night
                     do you sail
to sea on an ice floe
                howling sacred songs

O my lord, my good
                        dark beast
                                        how is it
I cannot taste you
                        wraith & shadow
tripleheaded
                        blind god of my
                                        spirit, you burn
blue flame on the
                        green ice, long shadows
lick at yr eyes
                        yr fur like arctic night
                                        the fire
of your song

I will circle the earth,
                        I will circle the
                                        wheeling stars
keening, my blue gems
                        shoot signals
                                        to yr heart:
I am yr loved one, lost from eternity
                                        I am
yr *śakti*
            wheeling thru
                        black space
I, the white wolf,
                        Loba,
                                        call to you
blue mate,
            O lost lord
                        of the failing hills

THE LOBA CONTINUES TO SING

I will make you flesh again
(have you slipped away)
think you to elude, become past
& black & white
as photographs,
          O I will
lure you into being till you stand
flesh solid against my own
        I will spread my hair
over yr feet
        my tongue
shall give you shape, I will
make you flesh & carry you
away, O bright
black lord you are, & I
your sister
        & magic carpet

Will you ride?

————————

O I tumbled here for you, I put on flesh
drew down this skull over my flaming light
        slipped on this shaggy pelt
to make it easy for yr spirit to speak to mine

As in that bright unclouded ocean where the stars
are not yet born, where you & I
slid, tumbling like dolphins
                        we cd not
speak each other's names,

        O you leaped
into the worlds, & I followed
did I not
        falling & shrieking
I solidified.
        Merely to look, my lord
once more
into your great
                sad beast eyes

Share this sorrow.

PART 3

Her power is to open what is shut
Shut what is open

Ovid

SOME SHAPES OF THE LOBA

white crow
in the snow
carrying dried
branch of dead hawthorn
the wind
sets it aflame

       she circles, screaming
       in white sky over
       white (broken) ice
       calling his Name

———————

white bitch
at an open pit
howling after the
slow-moving dead

they move
thru the jointed door
they spit
white phantom beans
on the dirty straw

she seeks to blend
to melt her glowing
substance into wraith-life
seeks to move
smoothly enough to be invisible
but they
smell the elf-light of her
hope, they elude, she is

dirty white dog
at your door

_____

Mistress Owl drinking
blood of infants left
alone on the hearth
Mistress of all
Disaster she cannot
mourn, each dawn
throws a white veil over
the past, covers w/ snow
all the half-eaten corpses
Each dawn
is quicklime stripping yesterday
to glowing
white bones & their shadows.

Her power is to open what is shut
Shut what is open

Her power is to fall like razors
on the fine wind of yr spirit
Still water
                  in the current,
                              unmoving air
that the wind blows thru;
hers is the fire that clings, but does not
consume, dark fire that does not
light the night.

Torches in her labyrinth
                              throw shadows
on ice-cut walls. Flickering stalagtites
cut out of garnet.
                  Her bower
lurks in the unseen muddy places
of yr soul, she waits you under the steps
of yr tenement.

                  She gleams
in the wildwood where you have not dared
to walk. Wild yew & blackberries
tight, dried meat
of skinny winter deer, these
she holds out, like a key.

Her door

cannot be found, it is close-shut, it crumbles
it wafts in wind. Her power is to raise
the pale green grass of spring, the pale wildflower
carpets which fly starward like primroses w/ dogs
asleep on them. Her power is in spittle
& in the lentil,
                    it rises like smoke
from the reopened furrow. She terraces the hills
w/ her glance, her white breast gleams
in mossy caves you remember where the smoke
curled on the greenwood fires

she is the wind you never leave behind
black cat you killed in empty lot, she is
smell of the summer weeds, the one who lurks
in open childhood closets, she coughs
in the next room, hoots, nests in your hair
she is incubus
                    face at the window
                                    she is
harpy on your fire-escape, marble figurine
carved in the mantelpiece.
                            She is cornucopia
that wails in the night, deathgrip
you cannot cut away, black limpid eyes
of mad girl singing carols behind mesh, she is
the hiss in your goodbyes.
Black grain in green jade, sound
from the silent koto, she is
tapestry burned
                    in your brain, the fiery cloak
of feathers carries you
                        off hills
when you run flaming
                        down
                                to the black sea

she is the scrub oak, juniper
on the mesa, she is joshua tree
in your desert, she grows
in cracks in the pavement
she tastes of sage, tastes bitter
as chaparral

she is born in tangled woodlands of kelp
she walks those slippery hills beneath
the waves; she rises again & again
from coral cities
floats glistening to shore on
turquoise seas

She lay
on the straw mat
in the warm room
thinking about love, all the
afternoon, at least
remembering, not thinking
at all. There was no wind.
Child voices in the street.
Sleep on her eyes, she lay
slightly absurd, headband askew
daydreaming, a silly smile
on her lips, her legs
akimbo.

LITANY

"I have been a black cat in a silver chair
I have been a curled fist in a glove"

I have been a fingernail in your skin
I have been a gold spike in the skull
I have hung, I have dropped from trees
I have dropped piecemeal from the strongest shoulder.

I have set the strong dancing
I have copied the soft in marble
I have distilled fire and scattered the bright drops
I stand in a spray of weeds

Do you sweat, do you rack your brain?
I am the lump of wax in your ear
I am the music that you cannot hear
The song you do not remember

I have been the pillow under your head
I am cold volcano in the snow
I am the gold sword in the sea
I drink your outbreath on the edge of dreams
where you wake, sliding and struggling

I am the cliff where you may not stand
The mountain where you cannot live

I am the madness in your children's eyes
I have been a porcelain tower
and a black tower also
I have been a graveyard these last thousand years
I shall rise, like the full moon, from that cemetery

The Poet Prays to the Loba

O Lady
the hem of whose garment
is the sky, whose grace
falls from her glance, who gives
life from the touch of one finger
O Lady
whose hair is the willow, whose breath
is the riversong, who lopes
thru the milky way, baying, stars
going out, O
Lady whose deathshead holds a thousand eyes
eye sockets black imploded stars, who trails
frail as a northern virgin on the mist, O
Lady fling your bright drops to us, emblems
of your love, throw
your green scarf on the battered earth once more
O smile, disrobe for us, unveil
your eyes

MADNESS OF THE LOBA

Is it the molten core of the earth
I am swimming in? I turn, melting
in some murkiness
                    trying again & again
to open my eyes. Is that your
hand, or a quickening chunk of basalt
some rock crystal precipitating
                                out of this pain?
Hold me. Can you hear the stream
under this stream? Thirty feet down
blind fish sing lullabies
                  · to empty shells.
I am petrified frog, working up
                        thru grainy sandstone
shells in my hair, eyesockets
filled w/ lava. The island women
fry their fish in them. O hold me
I am keening w/ the sharks, I shall
fly apart; hands & feet becoming
constellations. Do you grit yr teeth? Can you
still compass me about w/ those skinny arms?
Sorrow presses on my black heart, it
becomes a diamond, slithering
thru murk. Is this
loneliness? Can you count? Static
bursts in my eardrum, I turn, a whoring
centipede in your drain. Slick
black sleek head brown hands or your
white arms, again, as you rub me down

w/ warm mare's blood, shrieking, you are
some naked animal skull on kitchen
chair, the floor
curls round me, some tunnel I follow
                              down. Call
a taxi, I shall walk
into black hole where crystalline insects crackle
clear antennae gigantic, yr door
shd be black, though yr house
is red, I fall across
the threshold, fighting
for breath, it is necklace, seemly
ornament, agony
of size

DEATH & THE LOBA

now you are near
                    your breath
                            is sweet, I smell
it over my shoulder you are
                            golden & young, it is
lies
    & slander says
                    otherwise, I see
no scythe, no skeleton, no bony
skull, you are
                    who I dreamed, golden
lover / glowing
                in blue
                            sea-mist swirling, you are
alight in
            green vines laughing, skimming
                                        white stones
on azure sea,
                I dance
to you, smelling
                    of bayberry, holding
my blind head
                under my arm

Is he in bondage? Does he bow
unwilling, to her embrace? Her velvet claws
skid on his tender skin, her fur
cozens his (hairless) body. He shuts
his eyes. He is
Christian martyr swooning in arena
transfixed eternal mystic in the desert
    stigmata in his hands. He is
her stripling son, or brother, he is ancient
stony emperor who will
flay her alive. He stands
Satan to her coven while she weaves
her dozen around him;
                    leans
on marble column, broken
                       St. Sebastian
stricken by arrows she does not recognize.
Does he know
death from desire,
               passion from immolation? Her tail
knocks at his sides, her growls
are shaking in his brain. She smiles, she
crouches for him, raises
her haunch.

Belili Ishtar The White Lady Mother of All Living Cerridwen
    Olwen Blodeuwedd Achren Danu Nana Brigit Io Europ.
Amathaounta Branwen Athene Lamia Cyllene Artemis Isis
    Anna Minerva Venus Aphrodite Danae Cotytto Demeter
Cybele Kali Eurynome Inu Plastene Lakshmi Sarasvati
Parvati Uma Bhavani Hera Linda Cameira Ialysa Dione
    Circe Diana Alphito Ceres Albina Caridwen Cerdo
Cardea Jana Juno Carnea Cranae(the stony one) Pasiphae
(she who shines) Proserpine Bellona Hecate Rhamnusia Freya
    Mairne Mary(Sea) Miriam Rhea(flowing one) Acca Arianrod
Ariadne(most holy) Calliste Alpheta Hathor Morgan le Faye
    Sara-la-Kali Niamh Calypso Moiria Urania Ossa Achaiva
(the Spinner) Magdalen Ruth Sophia Daeira Semele Agave
    Michal Eve Lilith Sarah Callisto(most beautiful) Tamar
Ashtaroth Asher Druantia Helena Nephthys Sekhmet Binah
    Mara Eumenides Spider-Woman Tara Yemoja Don Morern,
Olokun Prajna Nut Oya Tiamat Maat She Inara Anat
    Neith Mother Hubur Ninmah Ninul Nisaba CanyonLady

THE LOBA OLD

With what suffering do I finally recall
what has always been known to me
to read as false these faces before the Face
ignoring the dark sun. Now I am old
how swim the abundant waters, fly to nest
in that final wind? Forty years it took
for the napkin to fall from my eyes; for me to hear
the voice of the First Man chanting from the edge.
Forty years, the napkin is gone, I find myself
once more, at the foot of the gallows.

I will vomit up the stars, I will shatter
the sun & moon. This cosmos, gilded cage,
I'll burst apart. Or else sit still
sit huddled with folded wings
till the Finger reaches down to lift me out.

Sit still, till I die of thirst.

PART 4

I have come to know myself
and have gathered myself from everywhere

I am a shadow crossing ice
I am rusting knife in the water
I am pear tree bitten by frost
I uphold the mountain with my hand
My feet are cut by glass
I walk in the windy forest after dark
I am wrapped in a gold cloud
I whistle thru my teeth
I lose my hat

My eyes are fed to eagles & my jaw
is locked with silver wire
I have burned often and my bones are soup
I am stone giant statue on a cliff

I am mad as a blizzard
I stare out of broken cupboards

CHILDHOOD OF THE LOBA

1.
not that he was not strong, but his gentleness
over-ruled the rest & he sang
& he bent & sang half-forgotten folktales
to the child in his arms

for what else is man
but to span, like a wrought-iron bridge
what but to bind
the sky, unto the sky

2.
his hands
close around the bars, as they closed
on the spirit of his wife, breaking her
coral necklace. here the flame
sputters low, it is not as if he forgot
the sky that tore like an arrow
thru his side.

3.
beating & beating against the vault of heaven
lapis tiled roof raised over turquoise & jade
& bitter jade, all turning on secret pillar
ivory or horn, all turning irregular
while the ram's horn beats the darkness & despair
shouts back the rising sun.

4.

moon glide on black mosses textured
pattern of sorrow; rough
lichen phosphorescent in gloom
where demons dance. bitter fruit
& out of season. plucked
tho none demand it. plucked
where white tree glows in the darkness
where the deer
eat dry grass thru the snow.

5.

he stutters; he spits wine
at white star-flowers glowing in the dark
he treads down ancient ferns
his voice
tears at your brain like sirens;
his eyes
trample your heart like the drunk hooves of fauns
on a rainy Sabbath.
his breath explodes; red light & black smoke follow
the concussion. you topple.
not that he is ungentle, but the prayers
he writes to law were breathed on another planet
a different time-space where the purple air
wove dreams around eight suns.

Some Lies about the Loba

that she is eternal, that she sings
that she is star-born, that she gathers crystal
that she can be confused with Isis
that she is the goal
that she knows her name, that she swims
in the purple sky, that her fingers are pale & strong

that she is black, that she is white
that you always know who she is
when she appears
that she strides on battlements, that she sifts
like stones in the sea
that you can hear her approach, that her jewelled feet
tread any particular measure

that there is anything about her
which cannot be said
that she relishes tombstones, falls
down marble stairs
that she is ground only, that she is not ground
that you can remember the first time you met
that she is always with you
that she can be seen without grace

that there is anything to say of her
which is not truth

FOUR POETS SPEAK OF HER

'she was, herself, the dweller in the shrine
Nemo & elsewhere & her priest it was who walked
sword in his hand. He was
He-Who-Must-Die"
                              "It was
cresting point when we passed
from mother-rule"
                    "The priestly king
must have died again & again
as tribe after tribe swept thru"

                    "I HAVE SEEN HER IN THE MOON
                    SHE DOES NOT SMILE"

'even then she ruled, the people
obeyed no other voice, she ruled
beloved Figurehead"
                    "consort of conquerors
& later concubine"
                    "as concubine
she was no longer Source
of the darker power. The priest-king sickened.
The land began to fail."

                    "I HAVE SEEN HER ON THE HILLS
                    SHE DOES NOT SMILE"

"the warrior became the Fisher King
  He-Who-Is-Saved
  by sight of the Grail"

                    *"jeweled cup.
The memory of the goddess in her glory
removed to another plane"

                    **"plane where ghost
dancers dance & buffalo range
where Pharaohs are immortal & eternally
make love to their sisters"**

"THERE THE GODDESS IN AMBER ROBES
              RULES OVER THOSE
WHO HAVE PASSED OUT OF HISTORY"

              Was it sake cups or wine they
              passed around? Hashish, tequila, bourbon, opium?
              Talk rose & fell, & stopped. Lightbulbs grew dim
              in the cold light of dawn. A Chinese scroll:
              four poets /
                        nodding out

A PAINTING OF THE LOBA

It is in a dark & gloomy canyon.
By the streaming lines of her hair we read
the maiden
                    landed from somewhere else
came down rather quickly in front of the Indian boy
whose terror is clear:
                              his quickly halted steps
                              his desire. The moon
makes the most of the scene, the hint of wolf
about her eyes & mouth. Is it
vampire as we know it? Werewolf
as in the Slavic hills? The landscape:
stone mesas riding the sands, wind
in vast spaces, says other.
                                        What forces play
that we call "Navaho witchcraft"?

———————

The white wolf lady dances on the hills
on the edge of black mesas under the full moon
stalks of yucca outlined on the sky.
I guess she sings, I guess her hunting song
is what we're listening to.

The mesas turn to mountains, the yucca
to ponderosa pine. They fall away
to high flat desert, bare except for sage
& still she sings:
she points her nose at the stars, she fills her throat
she plants her feet; landscape behind her blurs
like a moving scroll: the moon & she stand still.

DREAM: The Loba Reveals Herself

she came
to hunt me down; carried down-ladder trussed
like game herself. And then set free
the hunted turning hunter. She came

thru stone labyrinths, worn by her steps, came
to the awesome thunder & drum of her
Name, the LOBA MANTRA, echoing
thru the flat, flagstone walls
    the footprints
       footsteps of the Loba
           the Loba
drumming. She came to hunt, but I did not
stay to be hunted. Instead
wd be gone again.   silent
children in tow.

she came, she followed, she did not
pursue.
      But walked, patient behind me like some
big, rangy dog. She came to hunt, she strode
     over that worn stone floor
tailgating, only a step or two
              behind me.

I turned to confront
          to face
                    Her:
                              ring of fur, setting off
the purity of her head.
she-who-was-to-have-devoured-me
stood, strong patient
                    recognizably
goddess.
          Protectress
great mystic beast of European forest.
green warrior woman, towering.
                              kind watchdog I cd
leave the children with.
                    Mother & sister.
                    Myself.

LOBA AS EVE

I am Thou & Thou art I
and where Thou art I am
and in all things am I dispersed

and from wherever Thou willst
Thou gatherest Me

but in gathering Me
Thou gatherest Thyself

GOSPEL OF EVE

i am thou & thou art i

where tossing in grey sheets you weep
I am
where pouring like mist you
                              scatter among the stars
I shine
where in black oceans of sea & sky
            you die
            you die
I chant
a voice like angels from the heart
of virgin gold,
                plaint of the unicorn caught
in the boundless circle

                  where you confront
broken glass, lost trees & men
                              tossed up
on my beaches, hear me pray:
                              your words
slip off my tongue, I am pearl
of yr final tears, none other
than yr flesh, though it go soft

I am worm
          in the tight bud, burst
of starcloud that covers your dream & morning
I am sacred mare grazing
          in meadow of yr spirit & you run
in my wind. Hear the chimes
that break from my eyes like infants
struggling eternally against
                        these swaddling clothes

and where thou art i am

astride the wind. or held
by two hoodlums under a starting truck.
crocheting in the attic.
striding forever out of the heart of quartz
immense, unhesitant, monotonous
as galaxies; or rain; or
lost cities of the dinosaurs now sunk
in the unopening rock.

who keeps the bats from flying in your window?
who rolls the words you drop back into seed?
                              who picks
sorrows like lice from your heart & cracks them
                              between her teeth?
who else blows down your chimney with the moon
scattering ashes from your dismal hearth to show
the sleeping Bird in the coals, or is it
garnet you lost?

                  What laughter spins you
around in the windy street?

& in all things am i dispersed

gold fleece on the hunted deer.
the Name of everything.
sweet poison eternally churned
from the milky ocean.
futurity's mirror.   ivory gate
of death.
the fruit I hold out spins
the dharma wheel.
I weep
I weep
dry water I am, cold fire, "our"
Materia, mother & matrix
                        eternally in labor.
The crescent I stand on rocks
like a shaky boat, it is
the winking eye of God.

steel, from the belly of Aries.
Or that cold fire which plays
above the sea.
White sow munching acorns in graveyards where roots
of oaks wrap powdery bones of the devas.
There, suckle at my tits. Crucify
me like a beetle on yr desk. Nod out
admist the rustling play of lizards, recognize
epics the lichen whisper, read twigs
& leaves as they fall.

Nurture my life with quartz & alabaster
& drink my blood from a vein in my lower leg.
I neigh, I nuzzle you, I explode
              your certain myth.
I crawl slimy from a cave beneath yr heart
I hiss, I spit oracles at yr front door
in a language you have forgotten. I unroll
the scroll of yr despair, I bind yr children with it.

It is for this you love me.
It is for this
you seek me everywhere.

Because I gave you apples out of season
Because I gnaw at the boundaries of the light

but in gathering me thou gatherest thyself

daystar that hovers
over the heavy waters of that Sea
bright stone that fell
out of the fiery eye of the pyramid

it grows
out of the snake as out of the crescent:
apple you eternally devour
forever in your hand. I lock
the elements around you where you walk:

        earth from my terror
        water from my grief
        air my eternal flight
        & fire / my lust

I am child who sings
uninjured in the furnace of your flesh.

Blue earth am I & never on this earth
have I been naked
Blue light am I that runs
like marrow in the thin line of yr breath

I congeal
waterlilies on the murky pond
I hurl
the shafts of dawn like agony
                down the night

PART 5

He who listens to her
fearing for the safety of the city which is within him
should be on guard against her seductions

PLATO

Helen on the wall
not real, not eidolon
sung, shimmered as a shell
of tortoise, heart
of abalone, wind
in the northern spruce:

> *wield the power of the flame*
> *against the flame, what echoes*
> *black in the flickering light rolls*
> *small in the thunderstorm*
>
> *this is yr defense*
> *against me*

1.
breastplate of opal, have you? shield of onyx?
yr hand
shall take my hand, squeeze dry
this breast, still soft, tho milky, drink

the Source of Life as poison, die to it
flying forever from hypnotic greens
that whisper in my black hair, use the god
to hide you from the God,
                              SING ME
AGAIN to yr children, fill their ears

w/ my praise
                    in that hope to stop their hearts
to set up doors: oak, iron or myrtle
thru which I may not pass

none the less, wraith, eidolon or woman
I walk that wall; the wind
carries the night of my tresses thru the caves
& hollows of yr flesh; you whistle.
you moan like reeds.

2.
the gates are iron, they are set w/ ruby
four towers in the corners, I pace
north to east; I draw the dawn
I rip it bloody from the laboring earth

we shout; in pain & triumph / the stars
hide, at last, is this
sacrilege? I hold
the bloody dawn aloft, it screams
earth moans, I shout: unholy
trinity, Hecate & three-faced walking
east to north

wrapping the infant in my silver robe
shivering loveless. . . .

this is Helen's tale.

REEDGATHERERS: The Loba North

this is a song
of clouds & black hills
sunset behind black hills
we are gathering grasses
the song rises & falls
as the winds rise & fall

the waves rise & fall
so does this song

SONG OF THE DREAM-WOLVES

they are coming, the jackals
they are coming, the jackals
to eat
elephant-meat

two days ripe, it is
the way they like it, it is
it is sweet
it is two days ripe
it is
the leavings of wolves
it is
the ripened wolf-feast

LILITH: AN INTERLUDE

Red & white
Lilith & Samael, entwined
emerge from the abyss
red & white &
intertwined
like the nadis.

QUOTED FROM AN IMAGINARY JUNGIAN SCHOLAR

She flies over partitions on the
wings of a bat; while you
play cards w/ a stranger.
                              She bites yr foot.
She leaves, screeching at the sight of yr
silver & turquoise. The stranger melts.

Dank mirror, a gilded swamp in which you
sink. A singing parchment that bursts
                      continually to flame.
Kingdom of smoke in which swirl demon children
whining eternally for the golden bread
panis angelicus, they glimpsed
on a snowy mountain.

Whose mouth
sits on yr mouth
so that you freeze?
Who blew like cold wind
thru the broken window?
Who sits like sphinx on yr chest
                  & do you dare
win at her game?

Diamond, quartz, agate, it is labyrinth
that nothing seals. Not the crossed
human hairs over yr chilly hearth
not yr screaming eyes in the mirror, not fire
viewed over yr shoulder at the
dark o'the moon.

A handful of starchips thrown
at the windowpane. Something
brighter than sapphire, not so green
as emerald. Clarified turquoise.
It does not stop her, either.

The horned lady
stands on lions.
She is winged &
flanked by owls.

Or is she soft
hermaphrodite
holds you against his chest
you suffocate; yr cunt
pulses w/ weird, green hunger you wd not
acknowledge.
The deal she offers in her business suit
seems straight enough.

Faust too, he thought so.

Or she takes yr shape, she bites
yr old man on the shoulder while he sleeps
he freezes, hears yr heavy corpse
roll out of bed beside him, she whirls
in holy incense meant
to hold her in abeyance: even myrrh
don't stand against her softness

only, there is sand in yr heart
dank wet rags in the corner, a footstep
like slime, again, on the threshold.
He rubs his eyes.

Delicious the flesh she offers, like succulent
rare meat from the spit, her eyes
glint thru sacred, ancient letters in yr study
the candle gutters. Unholy
perfect presence; blank
window opening on emptiness as if
the earth had rolled at last
beyond the stars.

You roll, listing thru gummy sheets like ship
in an ocean of glue; tossed
from dream to murky dream in a room
where morning doesnt come.
O Lil! The apple at *your* hand, at least
putrescent wd long since
have gone to seed.

She sleeps on sheepskins in yr dining room
shoots smack into her arm, murmurs soothingly
of the glorious vegetable soup
                    she will make, tomorrow
the velvet pillow
under her head is torn, the lice
writhe in her eyebrows. You unpin
her rhinestone brooch, slip the fringed piano shawl
off her skinny shoulders, she sinks her teeth
in yr wrist.

all night long we
rock around the clock w/ that
steady, steady
roll, o baby, all
night long, yr
juice, or is it mine
(the seed
is *not* yrs, baby) redhaired
mama w/ yr
all night long, yr
steady
jelly roll

Oh Lil! You promised me secrets of mushroom & fern
elf language of mosses, you swore
that I'd hear yr blood sing, took me to burial grounds
where blue bones danced to bikers' radios
sank in a murky lake where I cd not
follow you. You promised
endless, perfect afternoons where wood
rots slow; where house falls to dust
in slanting light thru the redwoods, but left
w/ only the red glint of meat between yr teeth
red glint of yr lipstick, blood of muledeer & jackrabbit
on yr murderous black crossroads

I'm biting at yr leash, I'm plotting
a way out of yr cage, Ma Lilith,
tunneling underground, climbing over the walls
fasting, plotting, turning a deaf ear
to the tunes you put me to sleep with.
Aint yr woman:
Olympia, Augusta, Eleanor
of Aquitaine, I aint: I got yr
barb in my flesh, but I'll take it
with me, to somewhere else.

O taste the
rose-petal wine
sip at
the cock of the demon king
long shadows
in the short grass
wind
off a thousand lakes
egret
strides thru the salt marsh
light glints
off the bay—
is there quest
beyond these moments?

The Queen of Lies
great Maya
is combing her hair
Her eyes
the evening & the morning stars
span time

crystal pyramid w/ diamond heart
"shoe of the goddess"

She is not Helen. On every branch of the Tree
is her face. Cheetah. Owl. Locust.
Fly in blue evening. Higher you climb
the more she fills yr dream.
She is the bolstering Other, backside
of the coin. Underpinning of stage set
you love. Whatever play you're doing.
She is flying moon in the clouds
on all the foggy coastlines of the earth.

Where land touches water; where fire meets w/ air
where guts of earth burst out in coal, or diamond:
it is flesh, it is flesh, it is Lilith.   Interface.

Huntress. She in red sari
half stands
in the stirrups. Her horse
of jet, if jet were navy blue
her horse of dark lapis
rises. He is raised
by leopard beneath him. She
rides horse riding leopard.
She shoots straight down.
Her arrows
drive thru leopard skull.
They do not stop him, as he in turn
cannot raise the horse from the ground.

PERSEPHONE

for it is at dawn
we comprehend the night
& in the spring
Persephone remembers Hades
relives her winter sojourn.
she walks
moaning over dry & stony fields;
                              her tears
raise primroses
—IMAGINARY JUNGIAN SCHOLAR

And must I return again to that
long hell? Narrower
passages than my shoulders now
slide thru? Cold lord of definite
passion. I have just thawed
Have barely tasted fruit I brought to ripeness:
The pomegranate & persimmon ripe
just as I leave. I go. My footsteps burn
they melt
the icy staircase; as in spring when I ascend
my frozen flesh blasts snowflowers into life.
O desperate this love that calls me home!
to icy caves where black fire shapes the walls
and ecstasy screams thru unrelenting winter.
My love is there.
Not on this softened earth.
Not in the life I quicken.
But in the bowels of night where all my warmth
is lost in vast darkness of galactic air.

ISEULT ON THE SHIP

Is there other time
than too late / when we wake
enough to recognize Time
                is it not always then
too late?
            Does the beloved's breath
still mist the mirror?
            What balances
at the turn of sundial?
Dream within dream within dream.

exquisite as milk opal
                smeared w/ blood
(yrs & his)
while the worms work in the
                hollows of yr face
while the clouds fly
            across the wailing moon.

How sails strain / mast creaks
                this rain
cold as his kisses   my thin wrists strain
to tie me to this ship
                which arrives
does it arrive?

in time? that is
                too late
we recognize

this ship, his fierce arm
                carries me across
thresholds of water

he does not wait, too late we recognize
Sin: that we live misguided, we die
alone it might be

The waves
reach salty, well they will not have me
unless they have us both,
                    we engage
oarless in one more race
we beach
        breathless

        this wind
will tangle our hair
        graveside
this shore
rocks, more than the ocean

SONG OF HELOISE

from out of the body of fire,
        the body of light
out of the wind, *virtù*

the light that is in the mind
these essences
moving
        pale color
al fresco
        a homecoming   (clarities
from out of the passion
        crystal, spiralling

books open within the Word
                small windows
light within light
          "space is a
               lotus"

from the body of light
             like dayspring
ineffable breath

& out of the crystal,
                    the fountain
                              jets like sperm
quintessence

        how the flesh
            adheres
                in its
            passing

PART 6

The Seven Joys
of the Virgin

So, to know what she was like
You must come to a place in yourself
Where columns strive . . .

RILKE

ANNUNCIATION

the tall man, towering,
it seemed to me
in anger. I was fifteen only
& his urgency
(murderous rage) an assault I
bent under. I saw the lilies bend
also.   I had been spinning
flax: violet for the temple veil. I had just
gone to the well for water & when I returned
he was there. A flat stone. Towering.
                  Murderous rage
like the Law. They call it
love. His voice
was harsh, I bent, I tried to
evade.
Sound trembled in my gut, my
bowels
spoke w/ fear—
                the red tiles
shifted beneath me; a light
flashed from his eyes, his hand, the blue stone
in his ring & my bowels caught
w/ fear. He said
  "HAIL, FULL OF GRACE" I remember
my hand
found a psalter, something real, the smooth vellum
sunwarmed
under my fingers

the wind had stilled, the lilies
bent of themselves, my body
bent under weight of robes
white muslin gleamed in my tears
                    in sunlight
like a gold brocade
& my head too bent
under weight of hair. I fell
to my knees, I salted
the ground before me

He did not move, his voice
had turned to thunder, there was
no word to remember.   but Womb
        He spoke of my womb.
        The fruit of my womb.
Sunlight & thunder. I had not
        heard thunder before
        in such blinding light.

————————

the rose, the thorn, the thistle
the rose, the thorn, the myrtle
the lily, the thorn, the thistle
the lily & the myrtle
the lily, the rose, the thistle
the lily, the thistle, the myrtle

————————

The wind
bent the palm trees again
the room was empty

I stood again, as one stands
    after earthquake
my young girl's hands
began to spin the scarlet thread
    for the temple

VISITATION: Elizabeth & Mary

Not the trees remain,
        not black wind
out of volcanoes. Not fur
        leaping from heart
of weathering rock.

Yet they remain, they two:
Fire & firebringer. The torch
that is a sword.
                    Magnificat.

Not small woolly grass
        not furze
will cover us.
(yr belly leaps & mine is still as stone)
Not the wild prairie grass
        that hides
white antelope.
Shrill the wind, no reed
to catch it in.

            They walk. Cold air &
            icebringer. Theirs the first
            scorched earth.
            Their sandals. Scorched
            on glaciers

No more the dancing babes, the tribal fires.
         No more chinook
breezes from Eden cover us,
      no dates
fall into our hands from tall
    palms, the babes

have melted all.
Post-math of Noah: flood &
barreling trumpet.
Now the galactic barrenness shall come

AND NEW STRANGENESS BLOOM
         all nations
shall call me blest

AND NEW STRANGENESS BLOOM
         all nations
shall call me blest

NEW STRANGENESS LIKE RED MARTIAN FLOWERLIGHT
LIKE GREEN VENUTIAN RAIN
         gliding secretly
past the waning moon. All nations
AS WITH ONE VOICE

Never again will there be any human
they two, the last:
      fire & firebringer
      walking in charred sandals
            thru galaxies
      space walkers
            wilderness & voice

wind from our wombs freezes
    the Alpine meadows
THAT NEW MADNESS FLOWER
                    Magnificat
FRAGRANT AND HOLY AS SAFFRON HURRICANE

one voice all whirlwinds
    all nations
calling us holy
    bringers of desolation
calling us blest.

NATIVITY

> *The unbreakable fetters which*
> *bound down the Great Wolf Fenrir*
> *had been cunningly forged by Loki*
> *from these:*
> *The footfall of a cat,*
> *the roots of a rock*
> *the beard of a woman*
> *the breath of a fish*
> *the spittle of a bird. . . .*
> —THE EDDA

1.

Dark timbers of lost forests falling into my bed.
My hairs stirring, not asleep. Did they fetter me
with cat's paw, rock root, the beard
(o shame) of woman? They fettered me
w/ leather straps, on delivery table. I cd not
cry out. Forced gas mask over mouth,
slave. I cd not
turn head. Did they fetter me
w/ breath of a fish? These poison airs? I cd not
turn head, move hand, or leg
thus forced. They tore child from me. Whose?
What kind beast, near, breathing, what
royal hall or temple where I got this
slave flesh? Breath of a fish, the spittle
of a bird. So thin & slow. Seabirds cry at
full moon. But I. Cd not.
They fed thin soup & sour
reluctant milk. What prince

fathered this mite? Silence
sticky as cheese. Kind beasts around me: Women
who knew same outrage. Every child here
princeling, is shackled & numbered. We breathe
in our rags to keep each other warm.

2.
Horned, like a king he had come, I did not speak
of this. Horned & dancing, I did not
question. I lay on stone
as in the oracle. He hissed, I answered
He danced between / stone pillars
no language in common. It was
coupling of fierce reluctant blood. And free.

3.
How did I come, world-weary here to lay
this final seed. Tumbling thru galaxies of
ice to this
                yellowed crumbling room
There to revive
                    in loneliness
mark of the beast.
                        Pray this resurrection
does not end
            his dance

FLIGHT INTO EGYPT

stone force. Stone heart. I move
boulders along this path. Pursued
by cries of 200 infants
       each of whom
might have been the Christ.
       I do not know
which one I have carried away
       on this aging burro.

on this road the sun
       never sets, I sit on
       stone walls
that never knew cool mosses.
I sit
beside scorched trees. I sit
       on boulders
& the same blank arch curves everywhere
framing the picture
       It does not
keep off the sun.

THE RUSES: A Coyote Tale

Sometimes you take up the trap &
run with the metal between yr teeth,
   At times it is better to chew off
your leg.
   You have in this case to consider
the trail of blood.
   Sometimes for weeks it is better
not to eat, the meat is poisoned, but
you wait it out
   knowing the creatures are not
consistent, they forget. Or they will
move on. It is hard to explain this
to the cubs.
   You keep downwind, stick to
the water; journey in thick mist
or at the dark of the moon.

   There come the safe times when
we congregate in the snow,
   under large barren trees & each
of us is a flame.
   an offering to the moon.
   At such times it is unnecessary
to sing.

The Poet, Seeking Her

Did she sit all day on that donkey,
*   or by the door*
of some humble cottage somewhere
Did she wear that cloak you
*   always see her in & was it*
studded w/ flowers?
Did she smile calmly, did she smile
*   at all, did she raise her eyes*
her fingers steady, hands steady at her work
*   did she*
sew, or bake
or dream, book open in her lap, was it
Egypt or Galilee, did the sound
of many children float to her, was it
*   one child only*
Was she alone "two mothers,
*   & seven children"*
& they the Pleiades—was she always
the moon.

THE MARRIAGE AT CANA

window
it is
window   on pain
    where the moon was
bitter window on
        lees that splash
 a sea
of certain dregs,   old sorrow
under yr house

      splashing like waves
that wind drives
     to harbor
crook of haven
    full of stillness
    wine or water
    thick as lead
    in that
       moon's shadow

JULIANA

1.
And now, friend, I do not know
where this prayer of the heart
leads me. I fear it is
Satan whose black
fur shines in my mind.
Horn of pale, yellowed ivory
endlessly twisting.

Insistent, joyful beat of hooves
swiftness of wind

there is nothing on earth to compare.
No god vision
    ecstasy of light.
All that is dross
to the immaterial splendor
of that black fire.
Lord of the Winds.

Eshu. Black unicorn. Hoofs beat
in my blood. My eyes are cloud.

Hunger flashes like blue lightning, draws
me in. His rein
tightens on my flesh, his bit
cuts at my mouth.
His whip lashes me home
and all for love.
Lord of Black Wind, horrendous
Father of Dreaming.

2.

Red mist falls like a rain of
fiery snow. The field
transparent as this window,
this room
thru which I see
herds of his children rushing
like mustangs; turning
to find the fire in which they cry
so loud.

3.

O he mounts me, he has broken
            the mirror, has burst
the opaque air; he comes
from the far side of this agony
of thirst. Tantalising. He mounts
me & it is all pain forever
& end of days

dove, lamb, first fruit, cattle
I am all these.

rocked on the threshold

RESURRECTION

1.
O what have I spun out of entrails
what vision
of unsubstantial hope

       whose hag arms received
       dead Matter of the world
       whose wolf head devoured
       tough, bloodless corpse
       howling like pity w/ in
       unopening tomb

now wander in morning field
see dew
bright on the hem of
this ghost.

laughing in frail sun

2.
now am I burnt, sunblasted
dry as angels
now I am towering presences I feared
in human girlhood

I do not touch him, cannot avoid
his touch. I stare w/ his eye
from chasm of my forehead.
his light
sweeps me
I am burnt to powder

3.
O I am crouching
beast & seek to devour
this wraith as I chewed
sinew & bone   3 nights
it was hell   danced
in my veins

now eat ghost / incorporate
light.   no longer burnt
but burning.   spinning
sun / flung torch
cast from the stars.   he
shouts   NOLI
ME TANGERE   he blasts
unhealing force.   I
cannot
keep back,   I leap
thru flaming hoop

CORONATION

I have unfolded from this flowering crystal
to leap
onto the safety of the iron rose

implacable son sets weight of metal
on my immaterial head

o *he* is actual, it is now I
become wraith
                my flat tears drop
thru concentric
                crystal spheres
                            which start
at my feet

and I stand in these structures of angelic sound
alone as any woman in her doorway
in the rain. . . .

1.
The pain of wings is nothing
        to the crown
which presses on my 3rd eye

is his little church the rock
    on which I founder?
while the stars rush outward
        to darkness, must I
remain still?

Monumental. I lack
even the grace of that girl
who bent to angels.
Flexible limbs of my flight
  thru Egyptian desert

2.
O crystal spheres imperfect
        eternally promise
perfection.
They eat my joy, my heart:
  These ruthless globes
devour saviors
  (if Christ is dove
  then is he cooked & eaten)

Tipareth ground to powder
        blood & bone
does not tint
                their clarity
        (they clip wings)
The crown is made in their image:
turning of melted angels

Beyond in black environ
  Lucifer triumphant
Among expanding stars.

3.
Is this the end of my dance
  on the temple steps
Eight year old dervish who thought
  to shatter stone
with her fierce, virginal joy
O, I shall burst

Burst thru
Take now
    milke of the stars
    & rub it in my flesh
        like sabbath ointment

I will fly
Broomless, unarmed, unready
        I will fly

PART 7

true events move upward

GIORGIO DE SANTILLANA

This wolf is black. She does not
stand among columns.
She does not hand
   the
       white rose
       or the red to
       the two gentlemen
who flank her.

Look at her, she is about
to run a race.
She is about to run
circles around the sun.

She sits demure
telling the stars
      like silver beads
they glide
thru her motionless paws
they twist
  like ebony chaplets
      enclosing
golden secrets.

She is sleek
& perfect like the falcon
she stands
angular as maiden
    in a silk dress
coiled tight as the spiraling
          labyrinth
          w/ bloody
lamb at its heart.

She is poised, quivers slightly, prepares
to run circles around the sun.

THE LOBA RECOVERS
THE MEMORY OF A MARE

    small hooves
    the ankles fragile
    unsteady
    not rooted here

    the eyes
    anxious
    eyes of a doe
    who has been hunted
    but not w/in recent
    memory

who walked across America behind gaunt violent yogis
& died o-d'ing in methadone jail
scarfing the evidence

or destitute in Fiji wiring home for comfort
destroyed among oil lamps Morocco seeking dead fingers
old man in Afghani jail / pregnant barefoot & whoring
    who did we pray
    who did we pray to then

laid out flowerless in abandoned basement
blue stiff & salt injection
just out of reach

wrote lipstick "save yourself" on tin rail of furnished
        room bed
eloped w/ white slaver & died Indiana of unmentioned griefs
or in love again peaceful scrawled candlesmoke "there is
        salvation" triumphant on borrowed ceiling
while friends coughed in the kitchen

who left tapestries, evidence, baby bottle behind in Vancouver
& hitched to Seattle for the mushroom season
trailing welfare checks & stolen money orders
Chicago gangster in earrings who minded the baby

who gathered reed grass for the wicki-up, eating
        horsemeat steaks in Colorado dusk
the painted hills bucking & neighing, it was her ankles

    were slender
    it was her eyes
    were tired

oatmeal & grits while the old man
    naked in bed / read Bible / jerked off
& who was the whore of Babylon in the
    kerosene lamp of yr childhood?

it was her skirt
was greasy
it was her skirt
was graceful
it was her skirt
you clung to, till she fell
you fell

        & who now remembers her hands
working dye into cotton
slant of her green eyes / Sagamore cafeteria
who has tears for girls now on Route One, the babies
wrapped in a scarf / the green
                  always further north
                  further than you can walk

    her ankles fragile
    unrooted, she walks
    into the Wind

MY LADY, WE ARE BEING HUNTED
—TRISTAN

possibility we are poisoned, possibility
there is no meat on the table, not even bait
in the trap. possibility they've already bought our parents.
possibility we'll run out of water; the salt marsh
is rising; we are followed; they've clocked our meeting
possibility this is an ambush
possibility they are downwind of us,
they've photographed the house, tattooed the children
possibility they've marked the bread with hexes
possibility the moon is theirs, & netted
possibility the web of idea is upon us.
possibility we've lost this particular rumble.

> who stole the sword we bedded; followed the fork
> in the road where we left no footprints
> who swallowed yr amber, lady, while we slept

possibility we can hide here indefinitely
possibility that we shd cut & run

GUARDAVIAZ!

If you stood again framed, by window
     & dimly
the glass reflecting the waves of some
     distant Bay.
                No mist of
     horror, passion,
     guilt.   Howling of fox-spirits
in unconditioned ravine.   If you stood
on some bridge, silent, unarmored
if there were monkeys
                chattering in large trees
or bullfrogs singing while mist
overrode the moon.
                If I cd recover
innocence of silver on yr wrist

     will we pause
     only to listen for footsteps
     shall I bed you
     only on this edge
where lust is ash / & compulsion
drives bone against bone.
                Who are you, lady?
Why do I regret
hours in pastel gardens where scented drugs
might have sharpened our senses?

                    You are silent.
You strip fur / & feathered skin
from netted game.
You smile.
          O you are sword
thrust / wound
in my toughened flesh.
                    What can compare
w/ the sinewy grime
                    of our bodies?

AND SHE TO TRISTAN

1.
O it is not woods

I'd lure you to.   If they hunt us

let it be among stars.

Let our trajectory be wild & smooth.

O let us not
                break cover

2.
But for you the path does not lead
Beyond *nigredo*.
                    The quartered deer
in the thicket & hounds
at the entrails. Dark night of the soul
            you love.
Hence sacrifice. For which since boyhood
        you oiled your hair
yr limp
            you are so proud of.   Yr crooked smile
Nigredo. The dark wood
                        & the silent dogs.

You do not love
                    my silver, but its absence.
This is vigil.   & you sleep now at the furnace
When you shd watch.
                         When you shd watch.

I leave in a spray of stars.

O make Latona white. Smooth out her hair.

Lick at her eyelids.

                    Lay her on cracking ice

where the pole

            brushes the day star.

The Loba Addresses the Goddess / Or The Poet As Priestess Addresses The Loba-Goddess

Is it not in yr service that I wear myself out
running ragged among these hills, driving children
to forgotten movies?   In yr service
broom & pen. The monstrous feasts
we serve the others on the outer porch
(within the house there is only rice & salt)
And we wear exhaustion like a painted robe
I & my sisters
                    wresting the goods from the niggardly
                        dying fathers
healing each other w/ water & bitter herbs

that when we stand naked in the circle of lamps
(beside the small water, in the inner grove)
we show
no blemish, but also no superfluous beauty.
It has burned off in watches of the night.
O Nut, O mantle of stars, we catch at you
      lean   mournful
      ragged   triumphant
          shaggy as grass
our skins ache of emergence / dark o'the moon

In whose dream
did she beg forgiveness, in whose
did she die alone

For whom did she bend like weeds
under mistral; who found her
crumpled beside the sycamores

Who raised her from the streets, who
bought her on auction block; in whose
vision was she lashed to an empty boat?

For whom did she gleam
in elfin cloth / unchristian

Who tore thin wraps or cape, who
taught her shame; who was condemned
to go like her on all fours?

Is it She in flame at heart
of the Rose
                    Beatrice
in flaming cart
                         or Guinevere
in gallows wagon.
                              Whom do you hesitate
to join?
           Does she glitter
in faience / black
                          in the gold room?
Does she stand in starfire on
arch of stairs?
                     What is unfolding from
these preposterous stars?

THE LOBA, IN MAY

And yet, she knows, no one has loved her enough
    nor can
no one has glimpsed the windswept
    chasm, the trees
    bent or broken in storm
howling
    of raw ghost on dusty
    horizon, or seen
grace of her hands, fondling amethyst chips
    she knows
no one has guessed the affirmation
    w/ which
she now wears the marks of love, bruises
    like jewels on her aging
breasts, the secret fire
    white hot
    in virgin grottos whose waters
no one has drunk.
                Blue liquid light
pours out of her brown eyes
                        her great head
bends, to hide dreams that have not changed
under a hundred lovers. She waits
he-who-can-see-thru-disguises, she oils
her supple, 16-yr-old limbs
                    brushes
her thick hair . . .

The Critic Reviews Loba

Where is the history in this, & how
does geometry of the sacred mountain give strength
to the metaphor

wd she have us believe
that passion & shifting flesh enhance
proportion

where are the dates, street names
precise equations? Must we accept
that star clouds burst with feeling
Hermes dances
in blood & bone
                        no longitude given / it moves
  & breathless beauty
of circle & dodecahedron
                              form the mind's light
cutting lines of Force
  thru this quivering
  flesh seedpod /
                        Cosmos

THE LOBA PREPARES AN AMULET
FOR HER DAUGHTER

It was not fate she feared
or the blue-veined hands
revealed by Nut
at dawn / only
the overlooked:
one copper bug too many in the dunes
beloved sandalstrap / the clutch
of screeching harpy making a cloud
before Astarte's face.

Was for this: the fitting
of wheel to wheel, she prayed
safety of one
the rarity of promise

chalcedony beads
on a white throat / flashing
the stars into active protection
a fence / sheer battlement, blue quartz
to hem her round.

But we cant
turn it around. Turn. No way
no way, beloved, you can become
(for me) source. As I
for you, Muse, mystery. Those, the
elegant, long
fingers, traceries of the eternal
breath in yr touch, in the rhythm
of love. No way beloved that you
lead me home. So must I be
Place of my seeking as I am
ground for you. Spoor &
old trail lie on me, map
of my flesh. And Quest
ends for me (as for you) at this
not fresh Rose.

GUINEVERE

They pass as a second / they
have taken my beauty.

My hair grown thinner, the line
of my breasts / loosened.

Do you understand, beloved? It was
not yr hesitation, but the taste on yr tongue
when you stumbled
                & the stars crashed
around you.   Beryl.
                The cup
in the flame.   I cd not seek
the way to you, but only
                the way to Myself.

The way to Myself you sought
                it is not for me
to find you, planetary
                wanderer.

Ah to me
even when you paused
                on the edge of shame
to me you were golden
                golden.
It was not for me.
            to forsake the gallows cart.

To you it is given
        to seek the other / to me
perfection. Completion.
    The circle
I may not step out of.
        The black fire of yr flaws
consumes me.
        We are eternal.

We have played the time out / we
have paid the time. Have done
our time, beloved.   Done our time.
Do not pause again on this edge, lest I pass from
    the earth
unfinished & hungry
warped as a yellow ghost.
Come leap into light / the aureole
                                    surrounds me
be this coronation or hanging.   The stake
at Montségur.
For sweeter than shame
is the fire.

Antlered
I flee him
who wd crown me
w/ gold

what thicket shall keep out
the hounds of anger

PART 8

For disorder does not come from heaven
But is brought about by women

SHIH CHING

LOBA, TO APOLLO, AT THE FOUNTAIN OF HEALING

now dervish I slough off
pain, which is my claim to
commonality of woman

were we not killed, out of jealousy, run thru
w/ a black lance, every moon?
did I not burn?
stand naked in icy waters while willow twigs
tore my raw shoulders till the stream
ran red?
did I not carry my lord's corpse cased in gold
       (cased in lead)
barefoot thru every turning of that wood?

      I whirl
      to undo
      the winding sheet

      father
      mine, not yrs

was I not sold & sold & my daughters broken?
I remember
yr teeth on my half-formed breasts
welts on my legs. Have remembered
since childhood, carts of coal I pulled
in harness, wet of the mines, the leather straps
cutting my swollen stomach.

            can you laugh, father
            can you deny
            mouthfuls of blackened blood
            I spit out
                        each morning
            to sing?

now dervish I slough off
this pain which is claim
to womanhood.   Refuse

the remembering skin.
End commonality of rage
to be born
            in uniqueness.

HYMN: The Other Face

lucus
lycos
   grove of light
   thru which
   the white wolves
          glide
   silent
   their white breath
   flecking the leaves

     flat⟍   ⟋bluntness
          ⟩ planes ⟨
     spots⟋   ⟍of light

   footfall padding
      silence on silence
      white on white

thru trees of light
   light slants
      it spills
         on planes of light:
         forest floor

Reprise

Stumbled keening
   tongue cut out
        eyes . . . hands . . .
stumbled keening
           thru the forests of Provence
after the debacle of Montségur.

& still you expect
         we'll carry the sweet Grail
         out of those woods
         to yr table.

Table where I was chained, often enough
like a monkey.
        Or yr door, where it
   was decreed
I go on all fours. To carry
all guests on my back
         until forgiveness.
Forgiveness? O Lord of Measure
there is No Thing to measure
            w/out me.

        Do you growl?
        Know I cannot undertake
        to meet you, tho it be only
        a step.

Under this temple there is a well so ancient
it will abide the mouldering of the floor.
This night, for healing, I'll tear up
the flagstones; for oracle, drink

the black water
               Apollo
                 abhors.

FOR CAMERON

How was woman broken?
      Falling out of attention.
      Wiping gnarled fingers on a faded housedress.
      Lying down in the puddle beside the broken jug.

It is too easy to write this.
      Write of the grey
      in straggling, thinning hair.

      Write of the mounds
      of blue cake, under the moon.

Where was the slack,   the loss
      of early fierceness?
      How did we come to be contained
      in rooms?   Which room

holds the jewels which buy us
      & for which we have
      other uses?
      It is too easy

to grind our teeth in our sleep.
      Give me that porcelain jug
      too big to carry, too
      precious for you to part with

let me figure how to get it home
    unbroken. Give me
    that story you wear
    like a stone (jewel)

Or yr slack breast under my hand.

LIGHT MADE MY BODY TO LIVE
& SOMETHING BE ADDED UPON THE CROSS
WHICH GAVE TO FLESH THE QUALITY OF DYING
                    UNTIL IT LIVES.
DO YOU UNDERSTAND, PIERRE?
KNOW I WILL NOT BE STOPPED
                IN ANY DIRECTION.
OR EVER WIND TINKLED ICE IN FIRST TREES
THE MUSIC STARTED UP ON EVERY HAND.

ETERNITY OF TEMPLE FLOWERS
SPEECH OF THE DREAM.

Now born in Uniqueness, Join the Common Quest

I come to speak of the long & slender vase
of the goblet like a sphere laid open
of the vessel with two handles, the one with none

& all night the little waves
lap at the island village of Murano
mother of vessels

        I call to mind
severe white & black pots of Acoma
red clay of the Hopi
            drink the same wine
out of cut Serbian crystal, ruby tinted.

        What do you drink?
This is a foolishness. Who is the vessel?
Does the vessel drink?

and when we have won clear
we must return to the circle

Return
the hunt
to the measure of the dance.

Sweet friends
whose common dance
made Europe bright

when we have won clear we must return
to the Circle

Friend
that I murdered
in the sacred grove
            (grove of light
                delight
            beyond even the tongue
                of Wolves

or fled thru Asia
hiding in her caves

RETURN THE HUNT
TO MEASURE OF THE DANCE

Tympanum of pulse at bay
am I wolf or deer?
                    white hound
on a thousand windy tapestries

Sweet friends whose common dance
            when this you see

            When we return to the circle
            we have won clear.
            Return the dance to the pulses of
                        the Hunt.

LILITH OF THE STARS

for there is another Lilith, not made for earth
of whom it is said / that when she is seen by men
it is as a vapour / a plague / a cacophony
of unique bells / straining   & stranger, they pursue
her unsubstantial cors *thru this world*
& the next. She is, in fact, the archetypal
foxfire of the stars
will o'the wisp of empty space
cosmic marshlight that lures us away
     from the heavenly spheres, our home
to wander, forever, between quasars
at odds w/ the Sound of the Harmonious Crystals

temple flower of the abyss

                    windlass
                    on which is wound
                    that hope
                    which exceeds proportion.

Ship-That-Veers-At-An-Angle

White Fox that Leaps over Tombstones

BOOK II

PART 9

There is a way in which
I am a double of myself
my own mirror image
or that I give birth to myself
& am simultaneously
mother & daughter
like the double spiral

THE SECOND DAUGHTER: LI (BRIGHTNESS)

You enter power, but I am here before you
standing in what's left of grace on this planet
the bits shored up to form a circle of light
I cannot abdicate, even for you
           come, join us!

You enter womanhood, I am a woman
to greet you, invest you, praise you
(there are oils for your skin, your hair)
I have not grown old suddenly before yr eyes
      have not the courtesy to be decrepit
         small
      in the wind at my back & yrs
I have dances still to dance—do you dance?
      how the lights
      dance in you, eyes & skin
            & brights of yr hair
How yr anger dances!

See how my skin
        like yrs
            takes on its sheen
after lovemaking
         see how we glow!

The circle which is a spiral
stretches out
                    to the star of Isis
it is the stair of Light
                    in the upper parts   glow
the Grandmothers
                    laughing
The Ancestress reaches her hand
to draw us up.
                    She is white vulture
                        w/ spiral neck

      These years are the windings
of Light
      our flesh flickers & changes
like flame.
      Like flame, it holds us fast.

The myth of mother and daughter is not a myth of overthrowing (as in myths of the son & the father) . . . but one of loss & recovery. For there are realms & realms, in which the daughter rises to self-knowing, to equal status with the mother — & in the feminine universe, while some of the realms may be distant — "removed" — none is out of bounds.

—IMAGINARY JUNGIAN SCHOLAR

LOBA AS KORE IN THE LABYRINTH OF HER BEAUTY

THE LOBA SEEKS THE MOTHER IN THE INFINITE REACHES OF NIGHT

This is a journey to Egypt
Secret, prolonged, & varied as the paths
of planets out of orbit, brushed aside
                    by demon Chance
This is internal labyrinth of Nuit
                    her bowels
thru which stars fall to birth.

For all fall is the fall
                    out of bright twilight of her womb
to the dark & light
                    below

All things are possible within the mother
We differentiate
                         we lose the Chance
her demon son: splayed paths
                         spread like star's rays
The Roads not taken.
                         Opening to us
as She opens
                         shd we dare

This Road to blackest memory
                         the fountain
whence Egypt sprang
                         & powers of Sirius
Dog Star days that fell once on the earth

This is a journey backwards to beginning
Milke of the stars
                         first tentative slow days
when Nuit was virgin
                         & only Woman
                                   cd win her

the wolf Anubis
                         Opener of the ways
                                   She-wolf that climbed familiar
to that lap
            turning the faceted jewel
                                   then light
                                             now time
Splayed, raying, spinning path of Light
                         now frozen
Pathways of Time
            on which we labor.
                         Finite.

Beltain Note

"This road to blackest memory"

                       is azure

path of the priestess
leads thru
         the double helix

AULA LUCIS

He that knows how to wanton & toy with her,
the same shall receive all her treasures.
—THOMAS VAUGHN

How shall I win you to me? Shall I toy
w/ yr twat in the rain, in a dirty doorway?
Or draw sweet kisses out of
    yr twelve year old mouth?
Which is the blood, which the milk?
   & will you come
to press the secret crystal into my hand?

Oh this arcanum is crude
as sandstone gods
carved by the wind.
                Which star is formed of crystal?
Where do you move when fire
           blows from yr hair?
Are these yr favors
          & can I
survive them.   O sickly sweet yr love
like rich brown flesh.
          In which I wd bury myself.
Or the sulphurous springs that shoot from the red earth
          in steamy caves
fountain,
          whose echoing taste
          will not leave my mouth.
I have drunk direct at last
          from the cunt of the Mother.

The same shall receive
    all her treasures.

Endurance. What remains
in the gusts of thunder.
        How define
the limits of mutability?

Herbs pressing at the edges
of the moon.
        Desertion along the beaches

The shadow of a wolf's head on the cliff
What passes for innocence
child's gaze—the lifted foot—
the serpent, brazen, rearing

And this is a clearing in which glide   Spirit Wolves
Noiseless & dark
                              a little smaller than life
they glide clear up to my feet
                                        and disappear.
                              This is
a clearing in which the Beings gather.

who stand in my path
                              or stand by the side of the Path
while I make a circle.
                              The Ones, protectors
who stand on the far edge
                              & define what the boundaries
of the Haven are.
                              The Boundaries of Domain.

They are smooth as wolves   & the trees
are glad to see them.
                              This is a land
that has not forgotten its purpose.   Coexistence.
Love in Limitation   /
                              Spirit in extension
Interface.

COUGAR NIGHT REPORT

O he flashes purple
                    midnight
                              trembles
in the stasis of hope
                    wakes
on green ice
            seen from a plane
trembling in the nightmare
                          of a stranger's childhood

                    He
flings
        chipped flint
                      bends ashy
in permanent dawns
                    creeps laden thru hallways
                                              filthy
w/ image.
          Home?
                    Even pearls
can laugh
          at the sport
                      Soweto
falls as a tear

                    O he flashes
                                    emerald
darkness
            over nerves
                            of the desert
eats
            spider monkeys
                            abandoned in the arms
of joshua trees
                    the dawns
                                    tear pink
palmettos
            from his thighs
                                    while he spins
& spins
        by a thread
                        in the threatening
light.

TAHUTI POEMS

*For Tahuti is the true lover of Isis, and simultaneously and at
once, her child. It is Tahuti/Thoth who helps her restore the dead
Osiris, his incantations help her conceive the dead man's child,
and later revive the infant Horus after his death in the swamp.*

*Not the obvious: not Osiris, not Set. It is Thoth/Tahuti who
stands guard, who brings his magic to bear, Tahuti/Thoth, the
Magus, the Healer, the Ibis and the Scribe who is the hidden
(occult) true and secret Lover of great Isis. He stands behind her
other loves, and is her support, her daimon.*

IMAGINARY JUNGIAN SCHOLAR

1.

where he passes is transfigured
Light, does it learn

                     minutest

Color. Where he walks
Light bursts

        into blossom

a Mischief

        of possibility.

> *For there are greens that verge*
> *on purple, indigos*
> *shot thru w/ lights, magenta*
> *behind closed eyelids*
>   *when you are lost*
> *in the kiss of the Beloved*

As he moves thru/   Light
splinters

        into the Possible

Planetary junctures

               lost in time

return in time.   in Light.

2.

Tahuti

      Starfire

            Incantation where Despair

Breaks

      to the Manifest.

               All that has not been

Crystallizes.   Worlds

            precipitate

out of her tears

      at his speech.

           Song.

3.

Tahuti.

      He-who-prefigures

            Dawn.

Transfigures Light.

        New colors form

in the wind

      of his passing.

And the Dead Child

      stirs.

4.

Tahuti.

      Wielder of Image

                in the darkness

before Dawn.

          Ebb tide of Time

where the wet sand

              gleams   Phosphorous

& They rise

        sung to birth

              by his breath

Her low voice

         under him.

              They Two

under the worlds.

           Breathing

before the Beginnings.

5.

No lotus

       bears him ashore.

               No tale

speaks of his origin.

           He-Who-Is

in headdress

        or bird's head (mask)

Ibis /   or man.

         Smith, beater of runes

into metal.

        Hence, scribe.

            My lord.

He Who Walks

        staff in hand

             who chants

the unmanifest to Light.

           Whose spells

set the dead spinning

          Whose voice

penetrates veils

        beyond despair

         or judgment.

        Aeon

            whose Word

adamantine

       fills the Void

Tahuti.   He makes Black Isis shine.

6.

Tahuti, whose spells leap

                    serpentine

hissing like tongues of flame

                         in the shimmering night.

Who strides among crocodiles

                      whistles among reeds.

What babe that he does not warm

                       at his fiery heart?

Traveller.

          He flies over swamps of matter

skimming ground.

          He plucks her out of river mud

from the side

        of her scorpion handmaids.

And she is more than wife to him

                  They turn

like a double star

          past the warp

              of the world's horizon.

7.
He Who Was Not Born from a Lotus

It is the Word that is the Ground of love.
Master of tides.
                Pulse of eternal syllables that moves
between the stars
           viscous, shining web.
Gobs of spit
         from His mouth
                shimmering
seed of His cock
         netting void
            defining
Space.
       Vibrating song, the chant
out of his throat:
         Mantra that draws forth
star-stuff
     Milke that spurts
from her black breast at His cry.

Manchild who strides
        thru darkness.

8.
Human fledgling
wet feathers
            in cold wind
a whistle
            of pride
or power
            from his beak
spread of
            wet matted
                        wings
pinions
            of light/
                        in light.

Sun rises.
            Over the reeds.
The shapely mist.
                        Walking.
His keen eye.

PART 10

. . . as if Bear god
preceded Wolf god . . .

SACRED GEOMETRY

1.
cross-hatching on stone / & wind
flicking the light back
across the dolmens,   horses of the wind
riding in from the sea,   the voices
keening in full lament
                              "there is a blue
breaks on this steel grey
                              cerulean
breaks over azure"   the lashing rains
& the flesh
                quivering feast for the Riders
there is a blue
                models these greys, a fulness
as of flesh in the stone

2.
turning aside the lake for her,
flicking the page, as branches
turn in the wind
                    straddle time, stone cylinder,
& laugh.   legs falling away
                    astride uncouth & fallen
post.   battering ram.   time, bring
time
      thru the lintel, raise
the beams of the roof.   Rough
sandstone
uncouth carvings agape
                    thighs pressed against
carved *orgia* marking
                    the pink flesh, she rides
the cylinder backward
                    night mare
into the high
            wind.

3.
long hairs of the he-goat whip
in the wet wind.
                    haze
falls like a fine poison, hissing
the hills
            shiver & moan.   this winter
is like no other,   like no other
winter.
            goat stands braced to
the wind, his head to the north.
limbs of the trees are flying
                    thru the sky.

4.
remembrance of blue

her veins had shone like rivers
in her flesh,
             blue rivers active
in snowfields of torso,   she lay
sprawled on skins in the firelight
                  underground
house or barrows?
               no windows,   the smoke
curled like haze on hills, there was
a threshold stone they had both
clambered across.
              you cd slake thirst in her.

5.

snowflowers,   windberries,   dried moss the deer
cd smell,   thru the snow.

                             That was

another country.

             Here if the goat wd only

climb the fallen stones,

            or dance

about the dolmen

            It would complete itself.

6.

whistle into the wind.
                  Puck-
er the lips, stand w/ legs   wide for the Folk
to run between

             leap
as the boughs fly,   leap
as if over a fire.

            Is the lad fit

for her, another year?

            Or bring the black bear

to her cave.

7.

there are stone steps lead

                           from this place
to the edge of the sea.

                    they can be seen
when the sun shines,   they run
under the wave.

                when the sun shines here
you look on it,

                like the moon.
Clouds fly before it,   it races
ever toward night.

8.

the boats were not shaped like skulls,
but you felt

                that's what they were.
you could hear the clash of shields
tho no one moved,

                a clangor
above the wind.
As if a thousand women tore their faces
but dared not name the dead.

There were no dogs on this island
before they came.

9.
and the horses stood ashore, backs to the wind
and they raised a small round temple
                on the mound
it sank
                thru the winter,
disappeared in the spring.   They say Folk underground
took it to themselves.

When the sun shines full
                & you cannot look at it
It is then the white stair glistens

The bull
belongs to the moon
but he carries the sun
north.

Moon
is between his horns
but he carries the sun
in his belly
his blood. The sun
fills him up.

SHE WHO

she whose face we have never seen
she whose body is door to the world
she whose black thighs gleam w/ oil
                                    w/ fat & blood
she whose laughter is the earthquake
she whose inhalation is the end of time

who can compass her round w/ his arms?
who can penetrate to the depth of her desire?

stars are the seed pearls she sets on her flesh
they are the milk of her breasts & the juice of her love
her orgasm shakes the dark worlds to their depths

the lord of the dead stirs uneasy on his throne
he is one of the teeth of her mouth

her daughters stream w/ flaming hair from the portals of hell
they are the goddesses we can name, we name them Nut
we name them Kali & Olokun, Omphale & Mara

it is at their hands that the gods of men receive power

THE LOBA PRIESTESS AS BAG LADY
UTTERS RAGGED WARNINGS

don't
cheapen Aphrodite, don't sell
the objects she holds in her hands
don't
demand that she show herself naked
take
    the cloak
           along with her
welcoming
          folds of the Robe / she is
bright,   she is bright
              too bright
you don't understand
can't guess   have never
taken off
      your glasses
          these   strong
& cute stories of Demeter   will slay
like a boomerang,   don't
reveal
    the eternal feminine
kuntuzangmo   be
careful, a little   you are

so proud,   with your careful
tailored ways,   clipped prose
telling of Artemis,   of Ishtar
                    beware
the popular tales you like to
spread of Isis   will spread   like fire
like wildfire
          yr gut
has proposed itself for
calmer usage
        don't invite

tzuname / firestorm

Asher /
       Mother Mamaki

they have kindly
       robed themselves,   hidden
they are not

your toys

DEER LEAP

for Robert Duncan

1.

High hart at deer leap, park
to forest, the Law
changes utterly, rupture
of plane.   High hart moves sideways
across the path, his spoor
smells of fear, wind leaps
the deer leap, the law
in the park, formal, composed,
treacherous.   Who goes forth
to return? Wind
from the quarters spirals
in on itself.   The hart
fox or wolf, the beast
of the forest, sacred wood
                 spins
spirals or spins to a destiny
or brook, no hart can leap
over.   There drinks
reflecting.   Still.

2.

Wonder is light
at wood's edge, falling
reflecting green,   wonder
is open space where the forest
closes itself,   and nothing
protects or shelters.
Outside the forest, no law
shelters the beast of the wood.
No law outside   where wonder
sings limpid, glances
sideways.   Let us go then
love, where light
twinkles in the gap
between the Law
& ourselves.

3.

Darkling he follows.   It is as fox
or marten, his eyes are,
                              he has eyes
for the black green under leaves
in the small moon.   It shimmers
phosphorus, fungus,   the low
shift in the grass.   Dark he goes
into the light,   a flat
bent shadow it is joy
to see on the grass.   Come
love, what slivers fall
like flakes of light from a burning
tower they catch
in yr hair yr smile.   Winter
slips between our clasping
hands

4.

Do we break cover,   break
thru the small grass, bracken
is there light off the tall rocks
they stand far on the plain. We slip
from plain to plane, not daring
to turn back, we are far
from the white stair

                           what yr words
cannot say,   my tears
do not buy,   cuts a swathe
like the hare
              in tall grass
under the moon
                 we totter
aside to leap again
                 that hedge
or pass thru gate,   same flat
plain on either side
but the Laws   are different.

5.

sly as a marten,   evade
natural law   replace
one boundary w/ another, we flow
to its edge, roll back
define   this pain as content
rest-
        less as wind,   renew
ingathering,   to leap

sly as the shy
fox, remember, no law
protects the hare
                        from park
to wood to common
land he slips
                    always at risk
& always
                kin to the moon

6.

whisper my name, little Brother, whisper
across the Net that links the stars
                    where yr angel
buzzes like an insect,   hovers,
              the Rose
gives honey to the bees,   not cunt
          not heart or christ,   *rose*
is the soul,   yr soul
the angels suck at.   Oh love
light   displaced   making room
where gaps in the old
law
          flow like melting ice

7.

let us be what we are,   mid leap
let us fall or rise
on the breath the Will
                    yields to.
there are eyes
under all the leaves,   there are
lynxes, yes
            & the whisper
of passing shadow,   but the wonder
is there where boundary
breaks against itself
                    & the Law
shivers & bursts like diamonds
                    in the heart

PART 11

Another Part of Loba

And Loba is Lovha, or Louva
as in "Luv, ⚆,"   mitosis
which is Love itself
                    the wolf
is taboo, w/ the bear
the birch, the owl   because
because it forces
                    to *see*
bring the eye
to a focus of the semi–
or in–
        visible
                the hairs
of light around
or in lieu of
body   bright shadows
where no "body" as such
"is"
    (there are lynxes)
the air is thick w/
presence & the owl

eagle or wolf demand
our certain
            attunement

that we attend on
                    the passage

Thus Love
in wolf's clothing   stalks
like a hunger
the dark
researches of the
inland mountain

or flees
hunted   the thin knives
of

ravines
bristling w/
short growth   ravaging
as teeth
            of old men
sharpened
to desperation

wolf-form love
Vidal / toothless
Pound / faltering
Duncan   rage

thru inland   crevasse
for sound
of the sea   bent
in the flux

of fjord   thin whistle
of tides
thru the marsh

& love
in the stunted wood,   love

sounds its own

"we die
here
thirst
unslaked
die

but the moist
expanse

CREVASSE

every ravine a
glimpse

a narrow
door

or window
(we don't
move in
on it)

we don't
move
on.

The treacherous
blue mountains
walk
enfolding secrets

that lead us ever
farther
from
the sea.

From the wished universe
where flight
& lines of flight

vector
describing *itself*

as against?

as against
sunyata. Mist. The bark

or nightword

The wished-for
curve
of unqualified
flight

a blue
enfolding itself

arms of the mountains
crossed

on receding
dimension

A MANIFOLD

at last
a chain-link fence
we scale
like bandit children

Stealth of thieves
lest the spheres
close down

inelegant

beginnings
just out of reach.

Spilt milke
from a crystal
pitcher.

thus there is
no circle w/out feeling
the curved line
expresses the tension between opposing
(or at least differing)
wills,

The arch of the body
toward
& away from
itself

Light bends w/ its own weight
the heaviness
viscosity
of presence

The sticky nature of
void
a monkey business

dance of the creatures
in nets
& trees
of light.

But in the longhouse
the company are few

       sit or loom
       shadows w/ bright eyes
       geometries
       pointing outward

compelling the eye
to formality of function

Who goes?
What thought
moved like an arc
across the gap
(ravine)

The body itself is the vector
carried thru time
curve of the Will imprinted
on linear air

          (as if the full-dimensioned
universe
were the glass
of a Klein bottle   the substance
fluid / or gas
               it carries
another Order

To bring the whole form into silence
losing nothing
of the nuance of speech .

What does it mean to rot?
                    ——PARACELSUS

the light of the mind
like phosphorus
in the flesh
which opens, like a seed
            this is excess of water

desiccation
where the bones
rustle like leaves
on an old branch
betrays excess
of element of air

fire
delivers us to implosion
excess earth
to terrifying multiplicity
of colonies of cells
which swarm like ants

These are the vectors
we ride out of here

trails
out of the ravine
where sidewinder
& scorpion
herald
our passage
archangels
of the abyss

(where fire & water predominate equally
the body
overflows, or evaporates
like steam. Or,
kept at high compression
explodes
like the boiler of an engine.

A Note on the Above

Our death
belongs to Psyche
it is none
of the Spirit's
business

know the difference between epiphany & theophany
(sd the dream)

in epi-
phany the God
is outside

(to answer to

theo
     phany
           a
phanos of implicate

the *hieros*, even
falls short

             & *ethos*
             is not
             cannot be
             prima materia

             all "honor"
             is derivative

the arms   (branches
of the Tree
which shutter

△

□ not
earth

the Wind
do not reach

here

▽ not
demon
(daimon)

this gap
failure
to complete
the structure

○ not
heaven

we read as Guilt
(looking up

of Loba

the daughter is the Bridge
it is She
who comes again to heaven
& returns to earth

effecting a meeting of the
formed
        & the Bornless.

The harrowing of Hell
is the descent of the dancing hermaphrodite

Moon's darkness
not the underworld
Cerberus
a side issue

Malkuth
outside the scope of the
reaching Branches

& Earth is Hell
as the Albigenses
knew

an abyss
not marked on the charts

The city is built *around* the sun
constellated
& the fire central

THE INTERLOPER

Brazen
head
   (of brass)
or cinders.
Heaped on
"coals of fire"

People along
we don't want
along
sweet sister.

Unlikely
cargo.   Lopsided
harlequin
shapes

A "man" thinks
to dally
& come to
no harm

but the weight
of the dark.
It masses.

Rites of abeyance
cut a wide
swathe, sister.
Stand clear.

LOBA: The Winds of Change

bear ⟶ burrow ⟶ barrow ⟶ burrin

burnished,

it burns.

PART 12

Of man, the heart will remain
of the universe, the flower is indestructible

PARACELSUS

WALPURGIS

let
it lay. transparency
of earth. cores
of the dwarf stars
awash in black
light.   Spacious.
It is
enough.

The Loba Compares the Earthly & Heavenly Mothers

A corpse too gave me birth it was
harsh crevice of bony mountain falling
failing to hold me in a pouch or hand
Not the soft headwater of an inland river
bone dry. Out of dull twilight of her
eternal womb to
nest of hyenas, den lined w/ bone & feather
the lingering taste of soot & pewter / ash
on the eye, the tongue

We cried as from the bottom of a gully
& the harsh brush caught the sound & only then
if the will was sharp & elegant as crystal
did the Voice
ascend to the net of stars

THE MASK IS THE PATH
OF THE STAR

1.
stubs of horns
snout
huge eyes of
lemurs
              their language
geometry   these
we re-member
re-collect
              no *one*
is depicted here

2.
when all the masks are the same mask
that face
              a golden mean
writ in vajra space
              before
the birth of stars.

3.
and stars are buoys
                    marking
the paths of the sea.
reflecting currents / or
the currents follow star paths.

the whole thing a W — double mask
(double axe)   joined
at the forehead.
macroposopos
                        the double face
of the world.

4.
double gate.   the doors
swing silent.   and she
is Goddess of the Hinge.

5.
and the masks, finally, differentiate
no longer one face. We say
which myth are you living? we say
she belongs to the Bear,   the Wolf
the Toad   (Hekaat
            secret of Africk)
toad: the squatting woman
giving birth (Marija)   toad:
primeval
            transformation
done in the open   w/out cocoon
or pupa (Sheppard)

& Afrika   shaped
like a womb   /   like the bull's head
given
      in its Blackness
to the moon.

6.
It gleams.
Like the apes of Thoth,   their eyes
in moonlight.
                  Black ship of the world
whose language
            geometry
speaks w/ eloquence of every nuance
of the heart.

7.
we say, or said,   she belongs
to the Bear
the Mouse   /   the Turtle — now

we are lucky if we can name the power
she belongs
                to light   to darkness
we have lost
                nuance
fine angular line   she belongs
to the amethyst twilight
                        of the Dawn

8.
Usha.
"I go toward
                the Dawn!" cried Innana plunging
into the night sea
Erishkegal's house
                (but that was a different land)

9.
here   we have lost
nuance,   the subtle crumbles

        Like a house of cards
                        w/ all
the Trumps removed.

10.
but the Mask

         is the Path of the star
the Dogon say & it is true
lines of the Mask we follow

                (no *one*
                is depicted)

track on the air

         path of the psyche;   as our flesh
follows the paths of the sea.

11.
          & it is not
"nature" as such

            not sea of earth or sky
the Spirit seeks

            but the jeweled city dreaming
re-membrance
       re-collection

           when those Eyes
huge almond eyes above
           the pointed snout
emerged,
       & gazed the Worlds.

12.
concatenation of architectures prefigured
as crystal is
                the City
which is the Ramparts
                where all of space
is but one Park,   Enclosure
                common land
we graze in.

                I know
                        she said
She said
                I now *know*
There is an arcane Jerusalem

Ierusalem arcanum

which is the business
(& the word business brings us round again
to sea currents,
                        maritime buoys   marking
the unmeasured
                        the pathless seas

13.
arcane Jerusalem   /   *Ierusalem arcanum*
the only business
of the 3rd part
                        (or did she say "3rd half")
of the 3rd half
                        of Life.

14.
from the sea
                    to the mask
to the city in the sky

                    DayStar
we ride
                    toward Dawn.

15.
                    snout   /   & soft
rounded horns,
                    Light of the Mind
poured thru
                    lense of that Eye

we read
            as hologram

            "Eternal City"

[Dream of Emily Dickinson as Immaterial Surf Breaking]

w/out sea
a beach is "sounded"
tales of air breaking on air
the long strand, far as the mind
bright surf.
        Legend is land
under my feet & I stand
sun twice reflected
bouncing into the room
dogs weeping
          The dream
was of Dickinson,   waves
          crashing
la plage flat   GEOMETRIC
& all in the mind

PARTHENOS

the black stone shines tho its
color / clarity   we cannot
do not   name   & the door
swings soundless   hingeless as the
panel in his skull

                    who enclosed
claimed the war goddess

                            she who was
Owl in Africk   before
Zeus came out of the ground

The black stone
                    whose
clearness /   we dare not
enter   emits   a light
& the door swings   soundless
inviting   *its* light
is golden
            we know this tho the stone remains
inscrutable &

soft as the stone in
                    toad's head
Hekat
        frog-goddess   in what
was later
        Zulu

She who heals   thru darkness.

He enclosed   Durga, armed
maiden   cast her forth   his
headache   whose armies march
chthonic   whose destruction
takes place under ground
                              & she rose
feathers on her shoulders, a shadow
long as the road:
                    "Athena.   New beginnings."

Now death is in the light
                              it is
the light   golden   the door
soundless   the path   a silhouette
or outline of the Bird
the Owl, Hawk   all those
whose beak curves downward

Storms are bred underground   the sky
Revealer,   the
Interpreter   of what moves
in the earth.   Our dead
in the light of day
                            primary
lyke   before the sun
                            is created
rises   our Dead disperse
on the wind
                    as the hairs
of her feathers   move
her feathered shield.

First light is lightning   "worms"
dart thru the void   the arrows
before the storm

                we aver / the Raveler
whose helmet
                crests in plumes
a black wind
                flows out of them
brings pestilence
                the light
at her back
            the male-born
woman,   outlined
                black   definite

the path   she sd   is the body
of the god
            / dess
                    The death
she carries   golden suffused
inviting—her field is the
entrance point   the door
emits a mist
                miasm

pharmakos
            is the stone   it glints
green / golden / black
Her feathered skull   Athena
New
        Beginnings.

PART 13

Sun Wolf
shines on
harvest moon

The Memory of far things
is the continuous presence
in which I discover my Self.

Winds of change
bringing smell of the wheatfields
of graveyard, & swamp.

chance arrangement of constellations
cut in rock
                    the Knot
of Inanna we say now
                              gracing
the doorsills
                    we
are anachronism
                         time
stands still
              in the spiral
maze
         at the temple
                              gate

She has not left me   tho I have published our secrets
I have shown her face to the world, I have
spoken her Name.

The formula of love is the formula of Going
& it is the way of a god

Her translucent form stains the blankness
of the air
                    a luminous
transparency of color

She does not leave in her going, she arrives
continuously,
                    no epiphany

only Presence

GWALCHMAI

Whenever I am alone I find a fountain
And with it, often
a woman & a hound

Or stag.
The woman dressed in red.

When I am alone
the land reverts to faerie

These are diversions merely
      these adventures
of chess & hunt,
of battle / Sorcery

When I am alone
the fountain becomes the Companion

For me there is no
     Way but the Way
        of friendship
Companion.   Echo.

Parallel,
       the fountain
the victory
(lady in red)
are
consolation

is it
Consolamentum?

243

Companion.   Echo.
Parallel,
          the fountain
the victory
lady in red
are
consolation

of chess & hunt
of battle / Sorcery

When I am alone
the fountain becomes the Companion

The Echo,   Parallel:
the way of friendship

When I am alone,
the land reverts to faerie

These are diversions merely,
      these adventures

Whenever I am alone I find a fountain.
And with it, often
a woman and a hound

Or stag.
The woman dressed in red.

URSA

Blessed to be here in spite of
disturbing migrations of the Will
toward & away from

The blue bear in the kiva
                    & the bear at the pole
rotate on some other
pivot pin
            not what we thought

Blessed to be seated here
        at the center
the fringe

                neither the sky
nor the earth
                is enough
finally

THE LOBA IN BROOKLYN

1.

Her snout
pokes thru wrought iron
palings — gates
eternally closed

> Every man a seed syllable
> every woman
> its unfoldment (*padma*
> "you yearn toward us
> to see
>
> your own"

soft feminine face
(the snout)

> animal eyes

2.

what cd she buy
             w/ her passion   (suffering)
the fourteen way
                 stations
                      out of thought
in the abyss where even the glands
stop moving
             the crystal trembles
(almost) shivers
          she holds
                to some line or
principle she
          has no words for, only

that there are beings
          to be shielded   Those who wd break
under the scourge of reason
                 & she holds the line
some boundary unspeakable
               in pain   eternal
pain
   & not only
            for them

3.

To interpose my flesh between
insensate rage &

        the trembling,   well-ordered spheres.

To *be* the "skin of the world".

4.

Mars-fire burns in water
          does not rise

Or drown.
    Is not that simple.

5.

How wd I know male rage, he sd
except in those first 8 months
when I nearly starved?

        And a voice I cannot remember
rent the air
           informing my life w/ such
impassioned speech?

And sound *is* image
              it occupies
space,
    a shape
    cast on the brain,

Mars ripples the water
           we call it
           Sophic fire.

A PART OF THE THOUSAND WAYS
TO SAY GOODBYE
(Psyche to Amor)

Goodbye to the wings of light outlined
clear in the starlight,   the bare train tracks
rusting under the moon

who are you really

eyes
arch down as if from a tremendous height

yet I've seen you small
hunched
in mottled woods

goodbye
to the swords we carried bright
or chipped & stained
against
cobalt sky   the last
brown apricots of summer
filling our mouths the
brocade of
the saddle blankets frayed
        wind
plucking the cords

the plumes
of velvet hat quick smile
in formal gardens
your voice
              visible
a shade seen in the noon
light

        the alleys of Venice
        toothed lanes of Paris
        the roofs
        & dank port of Genoa   stone streets
        arching over our voices in
        Bologna   slick
        w/ tears   &   blood,   spittle
        of donkeys

goodbye
to the coolth of mica windows
set in adobe
long braids, heavy
pulling at my back
the black
waterjar in the shadows

goodbye
my life   (you are
my life   or anyway
my memory)
          I have been told
not to linger
          I wing

toward snow   or sun
to me
all light is cold   & fire
is in flesh
                  & stone
the full dance
of senses braided   I am

yours but
goodbye
to your   self &   my
unwinding here in the wind
of my haste   need

to obey   to follow
the stack of crumbling
paper   goodbye
even to the warm wood &
incense of shrine.   &   chant   I am
told to hurry   I am not sure

if toward death
or a further life

SUNWOLF: Beltain

Where else the cunning / strength
that, true of heart
      drags back the erring Sun
& not for herself?

Who secret goes the paths
      where the light has slipped
to draw it back abundant
in her pelt

        where the endurance
for this in-land journey
           whose heart
wd not crack
      at the leakage
of power from the world

but simply
      doggedly
          she goes the ways

(at least in the under-world
there is an over-

                    this wolf
travels horizontal
                    thru seepage of night

her cilia
          hollow,
          light vessels & her heart

becomes the sun
          she binds again to us.

HERMETIC ASTRONOMY

*The child starts w/ no other horizon
than the body of its mother.*
—JEAN MARKALE

1.
Sow yr gold
in the white
            foliated

Demeter
        is ash   is
ashes
      Isis
            all   fall

the white
sew
        Dione
in Leto   .
            Turn
in yr pointed
shoes

2.

Pointed stick
         forked
stick for plowing was first

dowsing rod
         led the dance

Led the Golden Bear   the
Sun Wolf
         in a spiral

These goddesses
            blaze
@ the turning of the Year
Cross (crow's)
quarters
not given to a masculine
sun

3.
in the white
foliated earth
not
    earth of morning

     this earth
has seen no sun

but the fire

          "Our" fire

golden Bear dancing
on a
short
tether

4.
womb is the land
the place
the sun comes from

womb
     the red jewel
Elixir
     (gold falls to birth)

Black friable earth — DIOS
White LATON
Golden Isis
     Sekmet / the One
who is a Lion

     she is
DEMETER is Hades translated
         Sekmet. Kali.

           She is
              the Ruby eye

5.

She is winter earth
&
Kore
     green

So the sequence moves
        (again)

toward gold

We claim the Sun.

PART 14

THE LOBA LONGS FOR REMEMBRANCE
IN THE BARDO

Shall we say that the streets were littered
                    w/ half-eaten food
dry leaves, debris of plastic & paper

Shall we remember the half-mad whores
                    who walked on them
Eyes black as Egypt : al-Khem
        the women
of that Night?

                              Shall we
recall the quarter moons of that era
their desperation
                the hopelessness of the wind
that flew out of Dead Center to its
                target in our hearts

What shall we keep of the hard shells
                    of our hands
the cloven claws held out to beg
                    held close
to keep what ran like sand?

Shall we be able to name the skeletons
ostrich & pachyderm

Who will remember the bleakness of this time?
Who will recall it, later?

EROS/ANIMUS

black body glistening, he stands
among vaulting tent ropes,
arch of canvas—

           oil or grease?
black light
     shines off of him
he is naked & yet somehow
somewhere
         is wearing red

his black eyes lift, or droop
almond or not
        they pierce
he does not move
he is everywhere

he flies
    trapeze or no
is Trickster Coyote   leaves
thru labyrinths w/ no center

he is
     nonexistent black wolf
mon seul désir
       his heart

in
  or out
       of his body

Her Dream

you are walking the streets of Omaha
w/ a husband, long dead
you are telling the aged dancer
who is crying by now
of boats to forgotten islands

& you wake
into a residence of the Mind
withdrawn,
textured

the title
Coming to Terms w/ Impermanence
is on your lips

"APPARUIT"

There is some sweet woman
whose words I have never seen
who springs
fullblown into mind

It is as if she had printed a large book
& her work was full & satisfied
& she
satisfied in the loves of both sexes
not strung out

by the *rappel a l'ordre*
not straining
or excusing herself or defiant
strident angry
not pushed out of shape

She has moved gracefully from fleshly maidenhood
to the lean delights of the mother

she is serene
with the grace & gentleness of the warrior
the spear
the harp the book the butterfly
are equal
in her hands

There is a woman who is full of grace
her lap is ample & empty
she is not abstract or sheepish
there are no tendons
straining in her neck

her voice is not milk & honey
it is not harsh, it is a voice
her voice   she writes

whatever suits her   she moves
where she pleases   she casts
a variable shadow

There is a woman whose poems are bread & meat
hyacinth   nightmare   crepe paper

I close a window, she is not reflected in it
but I see her silhouette against the glass

she is crisp as ice, is soft
as russian vowels

O sweet whore innocent
power my fiend
perfect fraud
you essence sniffing
my hand   yr inner ear
is the acoustic chamber
of stars
you commit
this poem like a ripe plum
I devour here in a desert
whose fountain   no caravans
stream toward

O shadow sister!

INANNA: The Epiphany

Before the first days, when no one numbered the moons
Before the first nights, when no one named the hills
When no one mapped the rivers, or set sail on the seas

From the steppes she came
From the place of tall grass she came
From the inland desert she came
She rode a lion

Arrows she brought with her, arrows
She rode a lion
A sword she carried, a flail
She carried the measuring rod

The rays of the sun at her back
At her back
She came to the sea

THEOLOGY BECOMES THE BODY POLITIC

The King is expendable, but not the Queen
The King of Sumer is expendable, but not
the Queen of Heaven.

Even w/ jewels on her eyes she cd not dream
of that casket in the wind

balanced on the edge of the battlement
                              where the hawk
flew.   She played chess.

He was chewing gum like any masked
dancer, squinting behind the veils

a fountain gushed in the
enclosed garden or was it Spanish

a patio clouds flew over?
a lizard blinked on the red

standing stone.
            What else is new?

Even w/ jewels in the wine she cd not see
the ship cutting a path to this place

Tho figures on the deck passed the goblet
to & fro in the pattern
                              of the labyrinth

She leaned into the sound.

Medusa Gazebo

blue babies birthing,
a thrown-away corsage:
orchids for Halloween, the
day of the dead
                she is fair brown
flesh for sale, for
                low bidders
in plaid jackets vaunting
                new age
patriotism of ghoul & shadow
country.
          Don't go too near the edge
             I want to tell her
I whisper it to her
         thousand tiny braids
knotted, at her neck
          she bends her head
looks at her cold tortillas, decides
to eat no more.

The Loba in Flanders

I am in the light &
the light rests on my hair
under a black cap.

I am crowned in red
my hands rest
upon my stomach. I gather

my red cape forward
my rings
catch light in a red stone

it is my black sleeves
wd gather you to my heart
to my swollen stomach

Is it
frozen flesh or polished bone?
This
head of a woman
like the prow of a boat
blind eyes
the hair blown back, face
thrusting into waters

carved out
&
polished to ivory

BEING IN LOVE WITH DARKNESS

1.
it shows
us off

we blaze
eyes
voice
bare flesh

the angle
of mouth to mouth

limestone is smooth
creamy
sparks blaze
like red &
fallen stars

star shadow:
strands of yr hair
against
the soil

In the dark
we are ears
& skin
mountain cat licks
the fur
of our charged
auras
lumen-
essence   seen
by all but human
eyes

2.
This is a gate between
black & white towers

heart of the pharaoh
awake
for centuries

blaze of mind,
a light
adjusting
masses of the land

3.
Why do I turn back, remember
spires & branches innumerable
wind in a skirt, or tunic
spears like fate, borne
away from the sheltering walls?

what grace do I still imagine
in cobbled streets, mockery
of shadow thrown across a
river, at sundown, blaze of stone
from the arches

Why wd I break for this beauty
thrown
like silk crepe over the limbs
of the world
& those limbs all granite
worn like flesh to wrench the heart?

How w/ this weakness match
& over match
imprisoned light
pharaoh or angel,   pyramid
or sand
encasing starlight for a million years?

Bears see only
summer stars.
This is important.

THE STARS SHINE FOR US

It was there that my heart faltered
There
That it let you in

There that I screamed   it was triumph
& death cry at once
        Here on the brink
of time as we once conceived it

screamed   shouted in joy & a rough
approximation of triumph
        There is joy in this
steady brightness
    backlighting the new dark

Here my hand was steady
    there it faltered but my voice
rang true
    Here hand & voice betrayed me
but I held
out of time to the clearness
        claritas
"unobstructed" \   they tell me
tho I have yet

    to experience

Here the tissue of lies, betrayals
    turned to gold
Leaving this edge   lead   brass
        so you could see
The process
        where it came from
if not where
        or how
it goes

This chipped corner
        missing bead   is the entrance
these three notes
        on the hurdy gurdy
define the elegance

        There is pride
in the going — & heart bursting
joy—
        The saints
go marching out—

        What
will you do, I want to ask, but I don't
when the last of them
        vaporizes in the heat
of passion?

        How will you
  measure
will you
  measure
        the dark?

ISHTAR

deliberate as the shell of a body you offer
ungainly on the steps
scratch of yr voice in the shadows
3 a.m.   gold shorts
& hot pink tights, high heels
& that ravaged face —
what are you selling, anyway?

deliberate yr limbs dislocated
awkward from drugs, you caricature
the human stream — enfold
the secret essence, perfect
bittersweet
tho it does to death — O sister
softer than watered silk
grey / white / black shadows of yr
ebony skin   yr heart
edible as chocolate   you enclose
the prize   & you know it

gate of death, encumbrance
golden morning of the world
you offer it   like poisoned silk
to the grinding, belching traffic,   hordes
of dirty men   like poisoned
watered silk
to wrap them round

Autour De

Do you understand?
There is a surround in which she runs long-legged, naked
w/ nothing to answer to

It is outer space more intimate than yr blood
Closer than marrow
Where she spins toward no ultimate

Where song never resolves into a major chord
& the light remains gritty
        bright beyond rods & cones
A medium thick as molten brass
        & finer
than spun filaments of aether

She is not mother lover sister maid or friend
in that surround she is greasy   terrible
        long-limbed & empty
common as broken glass

She reflects
        no light but her own

PART 15

KALI-MA:

"Versions" of Some Devotional Songs by
the 19th Century Bengali Yogi, Ramprasad

Because you love the burning grounds
I have made a burning ground of my heart, O Kali,
That you, Beloved, may dance there unceasingly.
Nothing burns in my heart but funeral fire
Nothing dwells there now but the ashes of the dead.
O Mother, who dances on Lord Shiva's corpse,
Come, swaying to the sound of drums,
Enter my heart's ash:
I await you with closed eyes.

You are the dancing youth in a circle of milkmaids
Your mantras are many
      your sports are various
What mystery is this?

Beautiful Radha is but half your body
You are both man & woman

you are naked
      your robe is yellow
your hair loose
      bound
you have a flute
      or sword
your glance charms Shiva
      your young male body
      draws the maidens to you

your laugh is terrifying, loud
      or it is gentle
you dance in a sea of blood
      or in crystal rivers

O Mother! I grasp the mystery!
I know you, Lady!

My mother is mad, my Father is mad, their two disciples—mad.
I too have become mad, meditating on the Mother:
Mad Goddess who stomps and dances on her Husband
who leaves the golden hills for cremation grounds.

Who can understand the secrets of this house?
　　　Like Father, like Mother.
And who but She would wear a necklace of heads?

Oh mind, you have lost the root
you seek after silver
Coins are a fraud. She is the treasure of gold.

O mind, you are unlucky
you wander about
The path of karma is irreversible.

Time grows in your heart like the shoot of a great tree
it will tear you asunder
　　　uproot it

Speak mantra w/ pure breath.

Make me mad, O Mother!
What's the use of knowledge?
Make me drunk with the wine of your love.
In this madhouse of yours some laugh, some weep, some dance
Jesus, Moses, Chaitanya—all crazy with ecstasy.
When shall I join them?
Heaven itself, a festival of lunatics—
                    master & pupil alike.
Who can fathom the games of love?
You too are insane.

"Thou art mad with love, Mother, queen of lunatics
Make me rich, beloved, in the madness of your joy."

When will heart lotus bloom
        the darkness vanish
When will I roll on the ground
        tears streaming from my eyes
as I cry Tara, Tara, Tara

When will distinctions vanish
        pain vanish with them

                say She is formless
                or that She is all forms

black Woman scattering darkness in the Dark

O the unmatched beauty of this dishevelled Woman
Her ravishing blackness!
Both gods & sages praise her complexion
Lord Shiva holds her color in his heart.
Krishna is also black, the milkmaids love him.
His flute & Kali's sword: one & the same.
My black Mother shines among gods like the full moon.

Freedom is born when the black forms blend together.
Shiva, Shakti, Vishnu, Ganesha, Surya: all the same.
All five are one.

Mother Kali! Madwoman! Get down & dance no more.
He is not dead, the great Shiva, he is in a trance.
You are strong, would have broken his bones,
                but he chanted your name.
Old Shiva is weak and tired—he drank cosmic poison
He is worn out by his long separation from you.
Do not kill him, who survived the milky ocean.
He pretends to be dead, to feel your feet on his heart.

Kali's greatness is increased by the One with matted hair
      & so we call on the Mother, day & night.

He is world Guru: as Shiva, as Rama
but even He does not understand Her
      He lies at her feet.

O Mother, put on a robe & cover yourself
& I shall place rose & sandalwood paste at yr feet.
You who are Kali at Kalighat
              Durga at Kailasa
              the beautiful Radha
              the milkmaids of Gokul
              dread Bhadrakali in the underworld
                    to whom the gods bring
                    human sacrifice
Where do you come from now, Mother? Who worshipped you?
Sandalwood paste on your brow, roses at your feet.
Your right hands offer safety; your left carry sword & head
You stride over mountains of demons & seas of blood.
      Your necklace: human heads
      Beneath you—Shiva.
      And yr gold crown touches the sky.

Mother you stand naked before your child.
You are mad, your Husband mad, the sages mad.
I too become mad with the hope of seeing You.

What woman dances on this battleground?
Naked Kali stands on naked Shiva.
Streams of blood pour from her black lips
ropes of blood cover her breasts and her wide hips
like red flowers on black river waters.
Her face is the full moon,
all the world's sweetness begins with her laugh.
Mountains of darkness dance together in her flesh.
My freedom is the fierce rhythm of her feet.

She is opposed to custom
She is shameless
She is immersed in joy
      she sways & smiles
She bathes in the confluence
      of the three great rivers
The sun & moon melt together
      in her flesh

Air blends w/ fire
All the world's aflame

Tara's name makes all prosperity vanish.
It leaves a torn knapsack
    & not always that.
As the goldsmith gathers gold & leaves the dross
    so her name steals good fortune.

O Mother, It is doubtful that your son can bide at home
when you & your lover sleep at the foot of a tree
    your bodies smeared with ash.

Tara encloses Ramprasad, you will not find him.
O friends & brothers! Forget me! I am gone.

I try to make an Image of illusion
Is She earthen?
I work clay in vain.

She bears a sword
    wears skulls
How can She soothe mind's pain?

I hear She is dark
    yet she illumines the world.
How paint that blackness?

Then too, She has three eyes:
    Sun, Moon & Fire
What artist could make an Image
    w/ such eyes?

She strides on the battlefield w/ loosened hair
Fire burns on her forehead
Her eyes are the sun & moon
Her transparent face shines like an emerald mirror
She is the color of a new raincloud

      She routs rakshasas
      Swallows elephants
      Leaps over seas & mountains in a flash

Is it a goddess, demon,
    naga or woman?
Her repeated war-cries pierce the sky

The Lady is fresh as jasmine
      & captures all hearts
She is naked
      her gait is slow
      her hair hangs loose
She is lithe & artless
      dark as a blue lotus
Her youthful face
      is the scripture of desire
"Deer's eyes and a lion's waist"

She has enchanted Brahma, Vishnu, Shiva
Who worships the sky-clad mother
      is dear to all gods

They call me drunkard, though I drink no liquor.
I drink her nectar only; my mind reels.
I sit day and night at the feet of Shiva's consort
High, not dulled with the wines of earth.
The cosmic egg floats on the elixir of her Joy.
She delivers the low-born, I shall not leave her side.
Virtue, ignorance, action, wisdom—these drugs delude.
But when you drink Her wine, you are out of tune
And the Divine Bard loves you: she takes you on Her lap.

I draw a circle about me
     w/ Kali's name
Then, listen, Death
     why should I fear your threats?
She is destroyer of Death
     the most mad goddess
Chanting her name,
     I throw dirt in your eyes.

I was drawn to this world
like a bee to a painted lotus.
In my greed for sugar I have eaten bitter fruit.
O Mother! you promised to play with me
        you lured me into birth
But all our play leaves me unsatisfied.
Well, that is my fate, I suppose.
But now it is evening, Mother, carry me home like a child.
Rock me to sleep in your arms.

The six systems of philosophy do not grasp her
She drinks devotion, She abides in bliss

At dawn She waits
             in your most secret chamber

Yogini lost in the ecstasy of love
             she draws the lover
             as the lodestone, iron

The days will pass; this day will pass:
Only our story will remain.
And generations of men will know your unkindness, Tara.

I have come to the world-market, I have shopped;
      I wait at the landing.
The sun is setting, Mother, take me into the boat.
The boatman fills his ship with the rich;
      I am left behind.
He asks for his fare, but I have no money.
O stony-hearted Woman! Pay my way!

The boat has left; the sun is going down.
I begin to swim in the ocean,
      chanting your name.

PART 16

She rises restless
from the worn
valley floor.

VISION OF THE HAG, DEVOURED

> *—the stars eat yr body*
> *& the wind makes you cold—*
> —LEONARD COHEN

even these teats, devoured
pitted by cancer, rutted
by nails of the occult beloved
      how the damned
      make me drunk
      w/ passion!

the bare flesh blotched
& pitted w/ poison

          the reek of breath
          from my stained
          & broken mouth

all this, O daughter
wylfen,
     my final lover
you convert

entwinement
  of serpents w/ a thousand mouths
&
  crushed & pitted
I remember
  Morning

je me souviens
  l'aurore

SABBAT REVISITED

The smell of carrion is the smell of birth
unspeakable flesh we eat
w/ the two-tongued one
graveclothes we deck
each other in /
   worm playmates
glowing — is this
necromancy? all phosphor
cold light of the dead & smells
of rotting leaves
   we dive thru
not in defiance
not to rouse disgust
because it is
      no horror
because it is

taste
      liquescent
      flesh
spread mould
pink green yellow on
these living breasts.
      under the ground
      in the water
      in the sky
cold glowing fires of death are fires of love
are eros
      stripped of a face

we fly thru cave
     thru marsh
     thru turgid
  ending lakes.

  We ride the winds.

TSOGYAL

The central nerve is a white
fire.   Do I dare speak
of this?   The whirling seed-
essence flares
           co emergence

the point
         where nothing has (yet)
been defined.

The horse of prana   rides on
the nadis
         I ride
that horse

But this is as nothing to the Voice

of the mantra
         rushing like breath
thru the thousand & eight

nerves,   voice of the Guru
flaring out

the dance I snake to the center
where bindu whirls
red/white
time/essence

so still
in this storm

Imago Mundi

Who stands in the sun?
who was meant
for these firestorms?

Address the blatant image of the world
Imago Mundi
where the sky vaults like a cathedral
not here.

      Charred pieces of her robe
fly by   on the fiery winds.

POINT OF RIPENING: Lughnasa

> *What Myth are you living?*
> —CARL JUNG

There is no myth
for what I am living now.

Nowhere does She walk out of the nursery
out of the granaries, the forest, the
circle of shields, to
wander
for Herself
scattering gifts as She strolls
to the Western Sea.

Scribe, painter, chanter of
new-made eternal
hymns, scattering pearls
of love, of healing — songs
books , dances , rites
pots, sculptures & piles of shells
of stones to mark
the trail (it is new)

There is no myth
for this older, ample woman

When she sets sail

                    poems on parchment
float on the waves.

2.
I wander   singing
turning in spiral
                  admiring
substance
            & astral roads

& neither here nor there

cross boundaries
                  gates
                        as of
                              worlds

is there a myth for a female
middle-aged
            Hermes
                        large breasts   not
quick-footed
            but
                  winged

            into & out of
                        dark &

                workings where stars
are sephiroth & there are
                              so many
                              so close

3.
(That rich time when the harvest
is not for yourself

You no longer need
to claim it.

Some myth that encompasses that.)

REPORT TO APHRODITE (Evening)

1.
In her service & not
in her service.   I tended
so many,   confused
Aphrodite   w/ Buddha

offended both.

2.
Finally taken ,   rapt in
brief respite
                    India
Egypt.   The power
of Amor.   Eros.
                              The Rose

3.

Defeated on all fronts,   I
opted for Mars.

        Constructed
& crushed
      worlds
         w/ an   elemental
    neither husband
nor lover   ,
       a parody
of Shiva.

4.

Who then was this
Adonis,   did he bleed?
Did   it matter?
      The bloom
lasts only until manhood

ripens.

5.
Gather

the hive
the Daughters
in one house.

The Rose
gives honey . . .

and the bee
                    is Yours.

6.
All these men's
sweetness
falters
sticks at your passion

stumbles
in riptide
beyond the breakwater . . .

ah, loves,   clumsy
& injured
was it not good
                    to drown

& drown again?

The girl had brought the weather with her
                                    —ANN LAUTERBACH

it clung like smoke around her torso
slowly dispersed
into the waiting void of the hills

cedar received the touch
of a kind of haze off her skin

the live oaks rose flame-like
out of the depths of her hair

       the wisps of clouds
        pulling out of her fingers
were purposeful, not languid as you might think

The girl had brought the weather it was
ambivalent,   it swam against the current

the sun
brushed against it, going down

ARIADNE AS STARMAKER

she draws me w/ a thread across the beams
& shuttles of her making
                                  static web
in which we swim
                              patterned ephemerides
unchanged
                  exploding instance

terrible freedom
                      in which the speeding quasar
& the camel
                  alike are still
in motion

                  the sound is of bees
the veil
            a net / the net
intangible &
                  inescapable

Boats sail on these lines
                                  only
                  stars expire
in this pattern
                      shimmering
                                  stillness

I am in chains for her delight
                love's body
the crossing of wills
                    multi dimensional
that forms the worlds

                She is the taster of the chained
enwebbéd
            face of things
                        She is
the web
        and all that's caught

                    She pleasures herself
in the binding
            & the loosing

We give her the slip
                to fly to an infinite
sadness
        clear as cold water

Is she also
            there?

PERSEPHONE: Reprise

one "life" is not more real than the other
not in "deflowering" do we come
into bloom; we have been always

there at the fluid boundary of Hades
we spring continuously into life & death
this is the province of the co-emergent mother
this is the daughter, sixteen, wrathful & ready

nor is the daughter separate from the mother
fruit within fruit; a sweetness
known only at the source where the fountain
                              divides
                              becomes itself
where fruit & seed & flower dance equally
exchanging shapes   exchanging essences

there is no knife can sever me from her
where I go down to bleed, to birth, to die

Sheppard Powell © 1981

DIANE DI PRIMA was born in Brooklyn in 1934. She lived in Manhattan for many years, where she became known as an important writer of the Beat movement. In 1965 she moved to upstate New York, where she participated in Timothy Leary's psychedelic community at Millbrook.

For the past thirty years she has lived and worked in northern California. There she studied Zen and Tibetan Buddhism, healing and alchemy, and raised her five children. She has also been a practitioner and teacher of western magickal traditions. In 1971 she began her epic poem *Loba*, of which Parts 1 through 8 were published in 1978. She is the author of thirty-two books of poetry and prose, and her work has been translated into thirteen languages. Her works include *Dinners and Nightmares*, *Revolutionary Letters*, and *Memoirs of a Beatnik* (Penguin).

She currently lives in San Francisco, where she teaches privately. Her memoir, *Recollections of My Life as a Woman*, will be published by Viking in 1999.

PENGUIN POETS

Paul Beatty	*Joker, Joker, Deuce*
Ted Berrigan	*Selected Poems*
Philip Booth	*Pairs*
Jim Carroll	*Fear of Dreaming*
Nicholas Christopher	*5° & Other Poems*
Carl Dennis	*Ranking the Wishes*
Diane di Prima	*Loba*
Stuart Dischell	*Evenings and Avenues*
Stephen Dobyns	*Common Carnage*
Paul Durcan	*A Snail in My Prime*
Amy Gerstler	*Crown of Weeds*
Amy Gerstler	*Nerve Storm*
Debora Greger	*Desert Fathers, Uranium Daughters*
Robert Hunter	*Glass Lunch*
Robert Hunter	*Sentinel*
Barbara Jordan	*Trace Elements*
Jack Kerouac	*Book of Blues*
Ann Lauterbach	*And For Example*
Ann Lauterbach	*On a Stair*
William Logan	*Vain Empires*
Derek Mahon	*Selected Poems*
Michael McClure	*Three Poems*
Carol Muske	*An Octave Above Thunder*
Alice Notley	*The Descent of Alette*
Alice Notley	*Mysteries of Small Houses*
Anne Waldman	*Kill or Cure*
Robert Wrigley	*In the Bank of Beautiful Sins*